Travel Guide To

PUNTA CANA, DOMINICAN REPUBLIC

Escape to Narbonne:
The Must-Have Travel Companion
for Your Adventure!

Wybikes Hinton

COPYRIGHT NOTICE

This publication is copyright protected. This is only for personal use. No part of this publication may be, including but not limited to, reproduced, in any form or medium, stored in a data retrieval system or transmitted by or through any means, without prior written permission from the Author / Publisher.

Legal action will be pursued if this is breached.

DISCLAIMER

Please note that the information contained within this document is for educational purposes only. The information contained herein has been obtained from sources believed to be reliable at the time of publication. The opinions expressed herein are subject to change without notice.

Readers acknowledge that the Author / Publisher is not engaging in rendering legal, financial or professional advice. The Publisher / Author disclaims all warranties as to the accuracy, completeness, or adequacy of such information.

The Publisher assumes no liability for errors, omissions, or inadequacies in the information contained herein or from the interpretations thereof. The publisher / Author specifically disclaims any liability from the use or application of the information contained herein or from the interpretations thereof.

TABLE OF CONTENT

Copyright Notice ii
Disclaimer iii
Table of Content..iv
INTRODUCTION 11
    Welcome to Punta Cana!.. 11
    About This Travel Guide. 11
    Why Punta Cana?... 12
    How To Use This Guide. 13

Chapter 1 15
Introduction to Punta Cana 15
    History of Punta Cana... 15
    Geographic Overview 16
    Climate and Weather 17

Chapter 2 19
Plan Your Trip to Punta Cana. 19
    Best Time to Visit 19
    How to Get To Punta Cana 20
    Visa and Travel Documents. 21
    Budgeting and Financial Matters 22

Chapter 3 24
Accommodation in Punta Cana. 24
    Overview of Accommodation Options......................... 24
    Luxury Resorts 26

    Budget-Friendly Hotels 28

    Boutique Guesthouse 30

    Unique Stays.. 32

    Top Recommended Accommodation 34

    Choosing the Right Accommodation for You................. 38

    Booking Tips and Tricks 40

Chapter 4 43
Must-See Attractions in Punta Cana 43

    Punta Espada Golf Club 43

    Indigenous Eyes Ecological Park and Reserve 46

    Hoyo Azul... 48

    Macao Beach 51

    Dolphin Island Park... 54

Chapter 5 57
Exploring Punta Cana's Natural Beauty............................ 57

    Saona Island.. 57

    Los Haitises National Park... 60

    Scape Park at Cap Cana. 63

    Bavaro Beach.. 66

    Horseback Riding at Uvero Alto...................................... 68

Chapter 6 71
Water Activities in Punta Cana 71

    Snorkeling and Diving 71

    Deep Sea Fishing 74

    Catamaran and Boat Tours. 77

    Parasailing and Jetskiing 80

    Kiteboarding and Windsurfing. 83

Chapter 7..88
Cultural Experiences in Punta Cana. 88
    Visit Indigenous Villages 88
    Local Arts and Crafts Markets 91
    Dominican Cuisine Cooking Classes. 94
    Merengue and Bachata Dance Lessons. 98
    Cigar Rolling Workshops. 101

Chapter 8..105
Shopping at Punta Cana 105
    Punta Cana Village 105
    Palma Real Shopping Village. 108
    Plaza Bavaro. 110
    Higuey Market. 113
    Souvenir Shops and Artisan Market 115

Chapter 9..118
Nightlife & Entertainment in Punta Cana. 118
    Beach Party and Bar 118
    Clubs and Discotheques 120
    Live Music Venues. 123
    Dinner Shows And Cultural Performances. 125

Chapter 10..129
Daytrips from Punta Cana 129
    Santo Domingo. 129
    Altos de Chavón..132
    Samana Peninsula..134

La Romea.. 138

El Limón Waterfall. 140

Chapter 11 143
Family-friendly Activities in Punta Cana 143

Waterparks and Amusement Centers 143

Dolphin Discovery. 145

Zip Lining Adventures.. 147

Pirate Ship Excursions... 150

Ecotours and Animal Encounters 152

Chapter 12 156
Wellness and Relaxation at Punta Cana 156

Spa Retreats and Wellness Centres...................................... 156

Yoga and Meditation Classes. 159

Beachside Massages and Relaxation 161

Nature Walks and Ecotherapy 163

Chapter 13 167
Historic and Cultural Walking Tours 167

Altos de Chavón Village Tour 167

Higuey City Tour. 170

Indigenous Eyes Ecological Park Guided Walk................... 172

Dominican Republic Heritage Tour. 175

Chapter 14 179
Itinerary and Sample Plans 179

Weekend Getaway Itinerary.. 179

Cultural Immersion Itinerary 182

Outdoor Adventure Itinerary.. 186

Family-Friendly Travel Itinerary 190
Budget Travel Itinerary 195
Solo Traveler's Guide 199
Romantic Getaways in Punta Cana 204

Chapter 15 209
Sustainable Tourism Practices in Punta Cana. 209
Environmentally Friendly Resorts and Accommodations 209
Responsible Wildlife Tourism. 211
Supporting Local Communities 213
Leave No Trace Principles. 214

Chapter 16 218
Safety Tips and Emergency Information. 218
Healthcare and Medical Services 218
Emergency Contacts. 220
Crime and Personal Safety. 221
Cultural Sensitivity and Respectable Behavior 222

Chapter 17 225
Accessibility at Punta Cana. 225
Accessible Accommodation and Transportation 225
Wheelchair-Friendly Attractions and Facilities. 226
Support Services for Visitors with Disabilities 227
Inclusionary Activities and Events 229

Chapter 18 233
Photo Guide to Punta Cana 233
Top Photography Spots 233
Catching the Essence of Punta Cana 235

    Tips for Smartphone and DSLR Photography 236

    Editing and Sharing your Travel Photos 238

Chapter 19 241
Traveling with Pets to Punta Cana 241

    Pet-Friendly Accommodation Options. 241

    Pet-friendly parks and outdoor spaces 243

    Pet Services and Veterinary Clinics. 244

    Safety Tips for Traveling with Pets 245

Chapter 20 247
Volunteering and Community Engagement Opportunities 247

    Local Environmental Conservation Projects 247

    Social Welfare Initiatives 249

    Cultural Preservation Programs 250

    Volunteer Organizations and Opportunities 251

Chapter 21 254
Punta Cana - Past, Present, and Future 254

    Historical Development of Punta Cana 254

    The Current Socioeconomic Landscape 255

    Urban Development Projects and Future Plans 256

    Protecting Punta Cana's Heritage for Future Generations .. 258

Chapter 22 260
Conclusion: Embracing Punta Cana's Charm 260

    Fond farewell to Punta Cana. 260

    Reflection on Your Punta Cana Experience 261

    Continue Your Journey Beyond Punta Cana 262

    Share Your Punta Cana Memories. 263

APPENDIX..265
Useful resources 265
    Emergency Contacts: 265
    Maps and Navigation Tools..266
    Additional Reading and References 267
    Useful Local Phrases: 268
    Addresses and Locations for Popular Accommodation........269
    Addresses and Locations of Popular Restaurants and Cafes. 272
    Addresses and Locations of Popular Bars and Clubs............274
    Addresses and Locations of Major Attractions 276
    Map of Punta Cana, Dominican Republic 280
    Map of Restaurants 281
    Map of Things to Do in Punta Cana 282
    Map of Museums...283

INTRODUCTION

Welcome to Punta Cana, where sun-kissed beaches meet blue waters, and swaying palms beckon you to relax in paradise. This travel book is your ultimate companion for discovering the beauty and mysteries of Punta Cana, a tropical sanctuary located in the Dominican Republic's easternmost district.

Welcome to Punta Cana!

As you stroll into the magnificent beaches of Punta Cana, you're met by a pleasant wind and the promise of amazing adventures. Punta Cana is well-known for its stunning beaches, world-class resorts, and dynamic culture, making it an ideal destination for those seeking leisure, adventure, and luxury.

About This Travel Guide.

This travel guide has been thoughtfully created to give you with detailed insights and practical recommendations for getting the most of your trip to Punta Cana. Whether you're a first-time visitor or a seasoned tourist, this guide is tailored to meet all of your requirements and interests, assuring a smooth and memorable journey.

Why Punta Cana?

Punta Cana's undeniable attraction attracts visitors from all over the world. Here's why Punta Cana should be on top of your vacation bucket list:

Natural Beauty: Punta Cana has some of the Caribbean's most beautiful beaches, with pure white sands and crystal-clear seas ideal for swimming, snorkeling, or simply soaking up the sun.

Luxurious Resorts: From extravagant all-inclusive resorts to boutique hideaways, Punta Cana has a variety of lodging alternatives to fit any taste and budget. Whether you prefer luxurious extravagance or relaxed elegance, you'll discover the ideal place to call home throughout your visit.

Exciting Activities: Whether you're an adrenaline addict or a leisure seeker, Punta Cana offers something for you. The choices for discovery and excitement are limitless, ranging from exhilarating water activities like parasailing and jet skiing to relaxing catamaran cruises and horseback riding trips.

Rich Culture: Immerse yourself in the Dominican Republic's rich culture by exploring Punta Cana's busy markets, sampling local food, and dancing to the irresistible beats of merengue and bachata. Visit cultural monuments and indigenous communities to learn about the island's rich history, as well as the Dominican people's warm and friendly character.

How To Use This Guide.

Navigating Punta Cana's variety of sites and activities might be intimidating, but don't worry—this guide is here to help you every step of the way. Here's how to get the most out of your trip with this thorough travel companion:

Planning Your Trip: Begin by reading Chapter 2 to learn about the ideal times to visit Punta Cana, how to get there, visa requirements, and money-saving ideas.

Accommodation: Chapter 3 discusses many types of lodging, such as luxury resorts, low-cost hotels, boutique guesthouses, and one-of-a-kind experiences. Find the ideal spot to relax and recharge after a day of action.

Must-See Attractions: Read Chapter 4 to learn about the best attractions in Punta Cana, including beautiful beaches, championship golf courses, historical sites, and natural marvels.

Exploring Punta Cana: Chapter 5 is your guide to discovering Punta Cana's natural beauty, with information on water sports, eco-tours, and cultural events that will make your vacation unforgettable.

Dining and Nightlife: Chapter 6 will pique your interest in Punta Cana's culinary scene, with recommendations for top restaurants, street food vendors, and lively nightclubs.

Day Trips and Excursions: Chapter 7 provides options for day trips and excursions from Punta Cana, allowing you to explore the surrounding region and find hidden gems outside the resort's boundaries.

Practical ideas: Chapter 8 contains practical ideas for remaining safe and healthy in Punta Cana, as well as information on cultural etiquette and respect.

Itineraries and Sample Plans: Whether you're looking for a weekend break, cultural immersion, or outdoor adventure, Chapter 9 has sample itineraries to meet every traveler's needs and interests.

Sustainability and Responsible tourist: Chapter 10 explains ways to travel responsibly and help local communities, including sustainable tourist practices and volunteer possibilities in Punta Cana.

Chapter 1

INTRODUCTION TO PUNTA CANA

Punta Cana, a tropical paradise on the Dominican Republic's eastern coast, greets guests with beautiful beaches, blue oceans, and a dynamic culture.

In this chapter, we will look at Punta Cana's history, geography, climate, and weather to give you a thorough grasp of this fascinating place.

History of Punta Cana

Punta Cana's history is rich and diversified, influenced by centuries of indigenous habitation, colonial control, and modern development.

Indigenous Roots: Prior to European colonization, Punta Cana was home to the Taíno people, recognized for their superior agricultural methods and excellent handicrafts. They lived in peace with the lush natural environment, fished in the many rivers and farming crops like maize, cassava, and sweet potatoes.

Colonial Era: On his first journey to the Americas, Christopher Columbus landed on the Dominican Republic's coastlines in the late 15th century. The Spanish swiftly created colonies, notably Santo Domingo, which served as the capital of Hispaniola. Because of its distant position and difficult terrain, the area surrounding Punta Cana remained virtually unaffected by Spanish colonization.

Modern Development: Punta Cana was a peaceful fishing community until the late twentieth century, when it was recognized for its tourist potential. In the 1970s, a group of investors identified the area's natural beauty and began building resorts along the shore. Punta Cana is now one of the Caribbean's most famous tourist attractions, bringing millions of people from all over the world every year.

Geographic Overview

Punta Cana is located on the Dominican Republic's eastern coast, on the larger island of Hispaniola in the Caribbean Sea.

Coastline: Punta Cana has nearly 32 kilometers (20 miles) of beautiful coastline, including soft white sands and brilliant blue seas. The coastline is lined with luxury resorts, boutique hotels, and private villas, giving tourists a variety of lodging alternatives to suit every taste and budget.

Tropical Landscape: Punta Cana sits inland from the shore, with rich tropical flora such as palm trees, coconut groves, and mangrove swamps. The environment is filled with freshwater lagoons, secret caverns, and flowing rivers, creating several chances for exploration and adventure.

Climate and Weather

Punta Cana has a tropical environment with mild temperatures, plenty of sunlight, and just intermittent rain throughout the year.

Temperature: Punta Cana's average temperature ranges from 25°C to 31°C (77°F to 88°F) year-round. The hottest months are usually June through September, when temperatures peak in the upper 80s to low 90s Fahrenheit. Even in the colder months of December and February, temperatures seldom fall below 70°F.

Rainfall: Punta Cana has a rainy season from May to October, with the biggest rains falling in September and October. During this time, light afternoon rains are typical, offering reprieve from the heat and replenishing the lush foliage. The dry season lasts from November to April, with little rain and lots of sunlight.

Hurricane Season: Like much of the Caribbean, Punta Cana is vulnerable to hurricanes and tropical storms, especially during the peak hurricane season, which runs from June to November. While the region has strong infrastructure and procedures in place to lessen the effects of storms, visitors should remain attentive and educated about weather forecasts during this period.

Understanding the history, geography, temperature, and weather of Punta Cana prepares you for an amazing trip to this tropical paradise. Punta Cana has something for everyone, whether you want to relax on the beach, explore the beautiful interior, or immerse yourself in the bustling neighborhoods.

Chapter 2

PLAN YOUR TRIP TO PUNTA CANA.

Planning a vacation to Punta Cana takes careful consideration of a variety of issues, including the ideal time to visit, travel logistics, and budgeting.

In this chapter, we will go over all you need to know to arrange a vacation to this tropical paradise.

Best Time to Visit

The ideal time to visit Punta Cana depends on your choices and priorities, as the area offers something different throughout the year.

Peak Season (December to April): The peak season in Punta Cana corresponds with the dry season, providing vacationers with sunny days, little rain, and pleasant temperatures. This time is great for beachgoers, water sports lovers, and those looking for a relaxed vacation. However, it is also the busiest time of year, with higher hotel rates and bigger people.

Shoulder Season (May and November): The shoulder seasons provide a combination of good weather and less tourists. While May marks the start of the rainy season, rainfall is often brief and sporadic, and hotel rates may be lower than during peak season. November is considered the transition month between the rainy and dry seasons, with comfortable temperatures and low humidity.

Low Season (June to October): The low season in Punta Cana corresponds to the rainy season and the height of hurricane season in the Caribbean. While temperatures stay warm, rainfall increases dramatically, raising the probability of tropical storms and hurricanes. Travelers willing to take the risk may discover fantastic bargains on lodging and less people at this period.

Ultimately, the ideal time to visit Punta Cana is determined by your weather choices, crowd levels, and money.

How to Get To Punta Cana

Getting to Punta Cana is quite simple, with various transportation choices accessible to holidaymakers.

By Air: The most frequent way to reach Punta Cana is to fly into Punta Cana International Airport (PUJ), the region's major gateway. The airport is well-connected to major cities in North America, Europe, and the Caribbean, with several airlines providing direct flights to Punta Cana. Upon arrival, tourists may simply go to their hotels via taxi, shuttle, or private service.

By Sea: Although less popular, some visitors may opt to arrive at Punta Cana by cruise ship. Several cruise companies have itineraries that include stops in the Dominican Republic, with some ships landing near Punta Cana. Travelers may arrange transportation to Punta Cana from the port, either via taxi or organized excursions.

By Land: For those already in the Dominican Republic, Punta Cana is accessible by car from various cities and areas. The most usual route is along the country's highway system, which connects Punta Cana to Santo Domingo, La Romana, and Bavaro. Travelers can choose to drive alone or use bus services provided by several firms.

Visa and Travel Documents.

Before flying to Punta Cana, be sure you have the proper visa and travel documents to enter the Dominican Republic.

Visa Requirements: Citizens of numerous nations, including the United States, Canada, the European Union, and most South American countries, do not need a visa to visit the Dominican Republic for tourism. However, before flying, make sure you understand the precise visa requirements for your nationality.

Passport: All visitors to Punta Cana must have a valid passport with at least six months validity beyond the length of their stay. Travelers may also be needed to show documentation of onward travel and enough money to maintain themselves during their visit.

Tourist Card: In addition to a passport, most travelers to the Dominican Republic must acquire a tourist card upon arrival. The tourist card permits passengers to stay in the nation for up to 30 days and may be obtained online or at the airport.

Budgeting and Financial Matters

When budgeting for a vacation to Punta Cana, you must consider a variety of expenses such as lodging, transportation, activities, meals, and incidentals.

Accommodation: Punta Cana offers a wide range of accommodation alternatives, from luxury resorts and all-inclusive hotels to low-cost guesthouses and vacation rentals. Prices vary according on the time of year, location, and facilities available. Travelers should conduct research and compare lodging alternatives to choose the greatest value for their money.

Transportation: Punta Cana's transportation expenditures may include flights, airport transfers, rental vehicles, taxis, and public transit. While rental vehicles provide flexibility for exploring the region, taxis and shuttle services are convenient ways to get to and from the airport and throughout town.

Activities: Punta Cana provides a diverse choice of activities, including beach excursions, water sports, cultural tours, and eco-adventures. Prices for activities vary according on the type of experience and operator. Travelers should budget for excursions and activities that they want to do during their stay.

Dining: Punta Cana offers a wide range of dining alternatives, from informal seaside cafes to sophisticated restaurants serving international and local cuisine. Prices vary greatly based on the restaurant and area. Travelers should plan their meals depending on their eating tastes and expectations.

Incidental Costs: In addition to scheduled expenses, travelers should account for unexpected charges like souvenirs, food, beverages, and tips. It's also a good idea to put away some money for emergencies or unforeseen bills.

By carefully examining these variables and spending appropriately, tourists may assure a seamless and pleasurable trip to Punta Cana without breaking the bank.

Chapter 3

ACCOMMODATION IN PUNTA CANA.

When planning your trip to Punta Cana, selecting the proper accommodations is critical to ensuring a pleasant and pleasurable experience.

In this chapter, we will look at the numerous lodging alternatives in Punta Cana, ranging from luxury resorts to low-cost guesthouses, to help you pick the ideal location to stay during your vacation.

Overview of Accommodation Options.

Punta Cana has a wide choice of lodging alternatives to fit any budget, inclination, or vacation style. Whether you're looking for luxury, relaxation, or budget, there are plenty of options to explore.

Luxury Resorts: Punta Cana is well-known for its magnificent all-inclusive resorts, many of which along the beautiful coastline of Bavaro Beach and provide a variety of upmarket facilities such as private beaches, gourmet restaurants, spa services, and championship golf courses. These resorts appeal to sophisticated guests seeking a luxurious and soothing vacation in paradise.

Boutique Hotels: For those looking for a more private and customized experience, Punta Cana's boutique hotels provide a distinct combination of charm, character, and comfort. These smaller establishments frequently provide attractive lodgings, excellent service, and personalized activities, giving guests a memorable and unique stay.

Beachfront Villas and Vacation Rentals: If you want solitude, space, and flexibility, consider renting a beachfront villa or vacation home in Punta Cana. These accommodations range from luxury estates with private pools and beach access to modest cottages and condominiums, providing a home-away-from-home experience for families, parties, and couples.

Budget-Friendly Guesthouses and Hostels: Punta Cana has a variety of economical guesthouses, hostels, and budget hotels. While these accommodations may not have the extravagant facilities of luxury resorts, they give clean and pleasant lodgings for a fraction of the cost, making them excellent for backpackers, solitary travelers, and those trying to stretch their travel budget.

Luxury Resorts

Punta Cana is home to some of the Caribbean's most magnificent and exclusive resorts, which provide unsurpassed comfort, service, and facilities within stunning natural settings. Here are some of the best luxury resorts in Punta Cana:

The Reserve at Paradisus Punta Cana: Located inside the enormous Paradisus Punta Cana Resort complex, The Reserve is a secluded haven of luxury and solitude for discriminating tourists. Guests may select between large suites and private villas, each attractively outfitted with modern conveniences and sophisticated Caribbean décor. The resort offers exclusive access to a gorgeous beach, private pools, gourmet restaurants, and a world-class spa, offering a genuinely luxurious getaway.

Zoëtry Agua Punta Cana: Located on a quiet stretch of Uvero Alto Beach, offers a serene and sophisticated atmosphere. This boutique resort provides an intimate and romantic setting, along with large accommodations, personalized service, and gourmet dining selections. Guests may restore their body and spirit at the spa, swim in the infinity pool overlooking the ocean, or simply relax on the pristine beach.

Secrets Cap Cana Resort & Spa: Situated in the private gated neighborhood of Cap Cana, Secrets Cap Cana Resort & Spa provides adults-only luxury in a breathtaking tropical environment. The resort offers exquisite apartments with own balconies or patios, gourmet restaurants, and a range of recreational activities such as golf, water sports, and evening entertainment. Guests may also enjoy relaxing treatments at the world-class spa or lounge by the pool with a refreshing beverage in hand.

Excellence Punta Cana: Located on a palm-fringed beach off the coast of Uvero Alto, Excellence Punta Cana is an all-inclusive luxury resort built for adults seeking romance and leisure. The resort has large apartments with own balconies or patios, three swimming pools, a full-service spa, and a selection of gourmet restaurants serving French, Italian, and Asian cuisine. Excellence Punta Cana's calm surroundings and dedicated service make it ideal for a romantic retreat or honeymoon.

Hard Rock Hotel & Casino Punta Cana: For guests seeking excitement and entertainment, the Hard Rock Hotel & Casino Punta Cana provides a rock-star experience unlike any other. The resort offers elegant suites with rock-inspired décor, a spacious casino, and a variety of services and activities such as live music performances, world-class cuisine, and a Jack Nicklaus-designed 18-hole golf course. Guests also have access to the resort's expansive pools, white-sand beach, and busy restaurants and nightclubs.

These luxury resorts in Punta Cana provide unrivaled comfort, service, and facilities, providing an amazing and sumptuous getaway to paradise. Whether you're celebrating a special event, honeymooning, or looking for a luxurious vacation, these resorts offer the ideal backdrop for leisure, romance, and adventure.

Budget-Friendly Hotels

While Punta Cana is known for its opulent resorts, there are also some low-cost hotels that offer decent lodgings without breaking the bank. These hotels have reasonable prices while still providing handy facilities and locations for exploring the neighborhood.

Hotel Cortecito Inn Bavaro: Located in the center of Bavaro, Hotel Cortecito Inn Bavaro provides affordable lodgings just a short walk from the beach. The motel offers modest yet pleasant rooms with important facilities including air conditioning, cable TV, and free Wi-Fi. Guests may also use the swimming pool, café, and 24-hour front desk service.

Hotel Plaza Coral: Located in Punta Cana Village, Hotel Plaza Coral is an affordable alternative for tourists wishing to stay close to the airport and enjoy the local region. The hotel's rooms are clean and pleasant, with modern facilities including air conditioning, flat-screen TVs, and private bathrooms. Guests may also enjoy complimentary breakfast, free Wi-Fi, and on-site parking.

Primaveral Hotel: Located in the center of Punta Cana, the Primaveral Hotel provides economical lodgings close to famous attractions including Bavaro Beach and Palma Real Shopping Village. The hotel offers pleasant rooms with basic facilities, a swimming pool, and a restaurant serving both local and foreign cuisine. Guests also have easy access to surrounding restaurants, stores, and entertainment venues.

Hotel Merengue Punta Cana: Located in the El Cortecito district, Hotel Merengue Punta Cana provides affordable lodgings within a short walk from the beach. The motel offers modest yet comfortable rooms with air conditioning, cable TV, and private balconies. Guests may unwind by the outdoor swimming pool or visit the neighboring shops, restaurants, and nightlife venues.

Natural Village Hotel Bavaro: Situated in the Bavaro district, the Natural Village Hotel Bavaro provides cheap rooms surrounded by lush tropical gardens. The hotel has nice rooms with contemporary conveniences including air conditioning, cable TV, and private bathrooms. Guests may relax by the outdoor pool, eat at the on-site restaurant, or visit surrounding beaches and attractions.

Boutique Guesthouse

Boutique guesthouses in Punta Cana provide distinctive lodgings with a touch of local charm and warmth, making them ideal for guests looking for a more intimate and customized experience. These small-scale establishments frequently include attractive design, personalized service, and a relaxed ambiance, giving visitors a distinctive and unique experience.

Villa Pappagallo Boutique Hotel: Located within the elite Punta Cana Resort & Club, Villa Pappagallo Boutique Hotel provides luxury rooms in a peaceful location. The boutique hotel offers large suites with exquisite décor, private balconies or patios, and modern conveniences. Guests may enjoy individual treatment, access to resort attractions such as golf courses, beaches, and restaurants, as well as a peaceful ambiance away from the masses.

Tortuga Bay Hotel at Puntacana Resort & Club: Situated on the gorgeous beaches of Playa Blanca, Tortuga Bay Hotel provides boutique rooms with a focus on luxury and exclusivity. Oscar de la Renta created the hotel's beautiful villas, which each have their own private pool, butler service, and personalized amenities. Guests may indulge in exquisite cuisine, unwind at the spa, or use the resort's golf courses, tennis facilities, and private beach club.

Eden Roc at Cap Cana: Situated within the private gated neighborhood of Cap Cana, Eden Roc at Cap Cana is a beautiful boutique hotel that provides elegant rooms, personalized service, and world-class facilities. The hotel offers big rooms and villas with private pools, outdoor baths, and stunning ocean views. Guests may eat at the hotel's finest restaurants, unwind at the spa, or discover the local area with selected tours and activities.

Sivory Punta Cana Boutique Hotel: Located on a private stretch of beach in Uvero Alto, Sivory Punta Cana Boutique Hotel provides a serene getaway for discriminating tourists seeking seclusion and leisure. The boutique hotel offers exquisite rooms with individual balconies or patios, customized service, and high-end facilities. Guests may enjoy exquisite dining, relaxing spa treatments, and private access to the hotel's gorgeous beach and swimming pool.

The Bannister Hotel & Yacht Club: Located in the picturesque hamlet of Puerto Bahia, The Bannister Hotel & Yacht Club provides boutique rooms with a nautical twist. The hotel offers large rooms and villas with marina or ocean views, contemporary conveniences, and customized service. Guests may relax by the infinity pool, eat at the hotel's waterfront restaurant, or visit surrounding beaches, shopping, and attractions.

These boutique guesthouses in Punta Cana provide a unique and intimate alternative to standard resort accommodations, with individualized service, beautiful design, and a laid-back attitude for a memorable and authentic stay in paradise.

Unique Stays

Travelers looking for a really remarkable experience in Punta Cana will find various unique lodging alternatives that offer something out of the usual. These one-of-a-kind accommodations, ranging from eco-friendly treehouse getaways to opulent overwater villas, promise to enhance your Punta Cana vacation.

Eco-friendly Treehouse getaways: Escape the city life and reconnect with nature at one of Punta Cana's eco-friendly treehouse getaways. These rustic yet attractive rooms are set among thick tropical flora, providing visitors with a private and serene respite. Wake up to the sound of birdsong, take in panoramic views of the surrounding forest, and relax in a hammock on your private balcony. Many eco-friendly treehouse retreats include sustainable amenities such as solar electricity, rainwater harvesting, and organic gardens, allowing visitors to reduce their environmental footprint while having a unique and immersive experience in nature.

Glamping Tents: Enjoy the best of both worlds by staying in a beautiful glamping tent in Punta Cana. These big and beautiful tents mix the luxuries of a hotel room with the excitement of camping, providing visitors with a one-of-a-kind and exciting lodging alternative. Plush mattresses, en-suite bathrooms, and private outdoor areas are all available against the backdrop of Punta Cana's breathtaking natural splendor. Whether you're stargazing from your tent's private patio or indulging in a gourmet dinner made by your personal chef, glamping in Punta Cana is an incredible experience.

Overwater Bungalows: Experience luxury and romance by staying in an overwater bungalow in Punta Cana. Perched above the Caribbean Sea's crystal-clear waves, these large and exquisite bungalows provide stunning views, direct access to the ocean, and unrivaled seclusion. Relax on your private sundeck, swim in your own infinity pool, or snorkel amid vivid coral reefs right outside your door. Overwater bungalows in Punta Cana provide customized service, gourmet dining options, and opulent facilities, making them ideal for a romantic break or honeymoon.

Cave Hotels: Staying in a cave hotel allows you to immerse yourself in the rich history and natural beauty of Punta Cana. These unusual lodgings, carved into the craggy cliffs of the coastline, provide a one-of-a-kind experience that mixes luxury with adventure. Admire breathtaking ocean views from your cave suite, relax in a stone-carved Jacuzzi, and wonder at the ancient rock formations that surround you. Cave hotels in Punta Cana provide a genuinely unique and memorable escape, thanks to its hidden setting, rustic appeal, and modern conveniences.

Floating Villas: For the ultimate in luxury and tranquility, stay in a floating villa in Punta Cana. These luxury rooms are nestled on the serene waters of a private lagoon, providing visitors with a peaceful and personal escape from the hustle and bustle of the mainland. Take in the magnificent views of the neighboring mangrove trees, relax on your private patio, and swim in your personal infinity pool. Floating villas in Punta Cana provide customized service, gourmet dining options, and opulent facilities for a truly unique holiday.

Top Recommended Accommodation

Choosing the proper lodging is essential for having a memorable and pleasurable vacation in Punta Cana. With so many possibilities available, it might be difficult to narrow down your selections. To make the most of your vacation, here are some of the top suggested accommodations in Punta Cana:

Excellence Punta Cana: Situated on a magnificent length of beach along the coast of Uvero Alto, Excellence Punta Cana is an all-inclusive luxury resort built for adults seeking romance and leisure. The resort boasts exquisite apartments with own balconies or patios, three swimming pools, a full-service spa, and a range of gourmet dining options, including French, Italian, and Asian cuisine.

Hard Rock Hotel & Casino Punta Cana: For guests seeking excitement and entertainment, the Hard Rock Hotel & Casino Punta Cana provides a rock-star experience unlike any other. The resort offers elegant suites with rock-inspired décor, a spacious casino, and a variety of services and activities such as live music performances, world-class cuisine, and a Jack Nicklaus-designed 18-hole golf course.

Zoëtry Agua Punta Cana: Located on a quiet stretch of Uvero Alto Beach, offers a serene and sophisticated atmosphere. This boutique resort provides an intimate and romantic setting, along with large accommodations, personalized service, and gourmet dining selections. Guests may restore their body and spirit at the spa, swim in the infinity pool overlooking the ocean, or simply relax on the pristine beach.

Secrets Cap Cana Resort & Spa: Situated in the private gated neighborhood of Cap Cana, Secrets Cap Cana Resort & Spa provides adults-only luxury in a breathtaking tropical environment. The resort includes large accommodations with own balconies or patios, gourmet dining selections, a full-service spa, and a range of activities and entertainment opportunities. Guests may relax by the infinity pool, play water sports on the beach, or explore the local marina and championship golf courses.

Dreams Punta Cana Resort & Spa: Perfect for families and couples alike, Dreams Punta Cana Resort & Spa provides an all-inclusive vacation in a gorgeous beachside location. The resort boasts large apartments with own balconies or patios, various swimming pools, a full-service spa, and a range of dining options, including foreign buffets, à la carte restaurants, and informal eateries.

Sanctuary Cap Cana: Nestled within the private gated neighborhood of Cap Cana, Sanctuary Cap Cana offers a luxury and exclusive refuge for discriminating tourists. The resort boasts exquisite rooms with ocean views, a private beach, a full-service spa, and many dining options, including a steakhouse, seafood restaurant, and beachfront grill. Guests may also have access to the adjacent marina, golf courses, and equestrian facility.

Nickelodeon Hotels & Resorts Punta Cana: Perfect for families with children, Nickelodeon Hotels & Resorts Punta Cana offers a fun-filled holiday experience with plenty of amenities and activities for kids of all ages. The resort has themed rooms inspired by renowned Nickelodeon characters, a water park with slides and splash pads, supervised kids' activities, and a choice of dining options, including family-friendly buffets and à la carte restaurants.

Catalonia Bavaro Beach, Golf & Casino Resort: Located on Bavaro Beach, Catalonia Bavaro Beach, Golf & Casino Resort provides reasonable luxury in a stunning tropical environment. The resort has large rooms and suites with garden or ocean views, three swimming pools, a full-service spa, and a casino. Guests may also enjoy a broad selection of activities, including golf, water sports, and evening entertainment.

Iberostar Grand Bavaro: Situated on Bavaro Beach, Iberostar Grand Bavaro provides adults-only luxury in a gorgeous Caribbean environment. The resort boasts luxury accommodations with ocean views, a private beach, a full-service spa, and many dining options, including gourmet restaurants and informal eateries. Guests may also have access to the adjoining Iberostar Bavaro Golf Course and other amenities within the Iberostar complex.

Majestic Elegance Punta Cana: With its stunning architecture, elegant suites, and multitude of services, Majestic Elegance Punta Cana delivers a five-star experience for discriminating tourists. The resort has exquisite rooms with Jacuzzis, various swimming pools, a full-service spa, and a range of eating options, including foreign buffets, à la carte restaurants, and beachside barbecues.

These are just a handful of the top suggested housing alternatives in Punta Cana, each having its own distinct facilities, ambiance, and experiences. Whether you're looking a romantic retreat, a family-friendly escape, or an all-inclusive resort experience, Punta Cana has something for everyone.

Choosing the Right Accommodation for You

Choosing the proper lodging is one of the most crucial decisions you'll make while planning your vacation to Punta Cana. With so many alternatives to pick from, it's necessary to consider your interests, budget, and travel style to choose the best location to stay. Here are some considerations to consider while choosing lodging in Punta Cana:

 Location: Consider the location of your hotel in relation to the activities and attractions you want to enjoy in Punta Cana. If you're interested in beachside leisure, seek for a resort situated along the lovely coastline of Bavaro Beach. If you want a more isolated environment, try a resort nestled in the exclusive gated community of Cap Cana.

Amenities: Take into account the amenities and facilities offered by each lodging option. Whether you're searching for a spa getaway, a family-friendly resort with water parks and kids' clubs, or an all-inclusive experience with gourmet dining options and entertainment, be sure the resort you pick has the amenities that correspond with your tastes and interests.

Budget: Set a budget for your accommodation and find alternatives that are within your pricing range. Keep in mind that Punta Cana provides a broad range of lodging alternatives, from budget-friendly hotels and guesthouses to luxury resorts and boutique properties. Consider the value you'll receive for the money, including the quality of rooms, facilities, and services supplied.

Reviews and suggestions: Read reviews and suggestions from other visitors to receive insights into the quality and experiences of different lodging options in Punta Cana. Websites like TripAdvisor, Booking.com, and Expedia provide reviews and ratings from genuine guests, providing essential information to help you make an informed selection

Special Offers & Packages: Keep an eye out for special offers, deals, and packages given by lodging providers in Punta Cana. Many resorts provide discounts, promotions, and extra amenities, such as complimentary upgrades, spa credits, or excursions, which may enhance your entire experience and value for money.

By considering these elements and completing comprehensive research, you can find the best lodging that suits your needs and tastes, ensuring a memorable and comfortable stay in Punta Cana.

Booking Tips and Tricks

Once you've picked the appropriate lodging for your vacation to Punta Cana, the next step is reserving your stay. Here are some tips and ideas to help you find the greatest discounts and make the most of your booking experience:

Book Early: To guarantee the greatest rates and availability, it's essential to book your accommodation as early as possible, especially if you're visiting during high seasons or holidays. Many resorts offer early booking discounts and specials, so plan ahead to take advantage of these savings.

Consider Flexible Dates: If your trip dates are flexible, consider altering your plans to take advantage of lesser prices and special deals. Midweek stays and shoulder seasons sometimes provide better bargains and less crowds than weekends and peak seasons.

Check rates: Take the time to check rates and offerings from multiple lodging providers to ensure you're getting the greatest value for your money. Use online booking platforms and travel websites to compare rates, read reviews, and examine images of the accommodations.

Look for Package packages: Many resorts in Punta Cana offer package packages that include lodgings, food, activities, and other advantages at a discounted fee. Look for all-inclusive packages or special specials that bundle rooms with extras like spa treatments, excursions, or airport transfers to optimize your savings.

Sign Up for reward Programs: If you often go to Punta Cana or intend to return in the future, consider signing up for reward programs offered by hotel chains and resort brands. These programs generally provide special discounts, advantages, and prizes for members, including as room upgrades, complimentary amenities, and points-based awards that may be used for future visits.

Contact the Property Directly: In certain circumstances, contacting the lodging property directly might result in better pricing and specialized service. Reach out to the resort's reservation office by phone or email to inquire about any special deals, discounts, or upgrades available for your vacation dates.

Read the Fine Print: Before making your reservation, be sure to read the fine print and understand the terms and conditions of your booking, including cancellation policies, deposit requirements, and any additional fees or penalties. This can help you prevent any shocks or unnecessary fees later on.

Consider Travel Insurance: Protect your investment by considering travel insurance when reserving your lodging. Travel insurance can give coverage for unforeseen situations, such as trip cancellations, delays, or medical crises, providing you peace of mind throughout your travels.

Check for Additional Fees: Be aware of any additional fees or charges that may apply to your booking, such as resort fees, taxes, or service costs. These costs can vary based on the resort and may not always be included in the initial booking price, so be sure to incorporate them into your budget when planning your vacation.

Keep an Eye on bargains and Promotions: Stay updated on bargains, promotions, and last-minute specials from lodging providers in Punta Cana by signing up for email newsletters, following them on social media, or checking their websites periodically. Many resorts offer unique discounts and flash deals to subscribers and followers, so you may catch a terrific deal if you're fast to act.

By following these booking tips and tactics, you may acquire the greatest hotel options at the best costs for your trip to Punta Cana, ensuring a comfortable and pleasurable stay from start to finish.

Chapter 4

MUST-SEE ATTRACTIONS IN PUNTA CANA

Punta Cana, located on the eastern coast of the Dominican Republic, is famed for its gorgeous beaches, turquoise seas, and opulent resorts. However, beyond the sandy sands and luxury lodgings, Punta Cana provides a multitude of must-see attractions that cater to varied interests, from golf fanatics to nature lovers.

In this chapter, we will explore three prominent sites that are likely to enthrall visitors: Punta Espada Golf Club, Indigenous Eyes Ecological Park & Reserve, and Hoyo Azul.

Punta Espada Golf Club

Nestled along the magnificent shoreline of Punta Cana, Punta Espada Golf Club is a world-class golf destination that routinely ranks among the best courses in the Caribbean. Designed by the famous Jack Nicklaus, this championship course offers an unmatched golfing experience among magnificent tropical landscape.

History and Design

Opened in 2006, Punta Espada Golf Club soon received attention for its tough layout and scenic surroundings. Jack Nicklaus, widely referred to as the "Golden Bear," painstakingly built the course to accentuate the natural beauty of the Dominican Republic while delivering a demanding yet entertaining game of golf for players of all ability levels.

The course offers lush fairways, significant elevation changes, and expertly placed bunkers and water hazards, offering a memorable and enjoyable golfing experience. With eight holes playing along the dazzling Caribbean Sea, players are treated to stunning ocean vistas at every turn.

Signature Holes

One of the major aspects of Punta Espada Golf Club is its collection of iconic holes, each having its own distinct set of difficulties and magnificent vistas. Among these, the par-3 13th hole stands out as one of the most remarkable. Named "Punta Espada," this hole forces golfers to maneuver a tee shot over the beautiful seas of the Caribbean to a green perched on the edge of a cliff, giving a thrilling test of accuracy and nerve.

Another legendary hole is the par-5 18th, known as "El Codo Del Diablo" or "The Devil's Elbow." This dramatic closing hole has a dogleg left that follows the shoreline, inviting golfers to take on the ocean's edge with their approach shot. With the sound of waves breaking against the rocky beach as a backdrop, the 18th hole gives a fitting end to a spectacular round of golf.

Facilities and Amenities

In addition to its world-class golf course, Punta Espada Golf Club offers a number of amenities to improve the golfer's experience. The clubhouse contains elegant locker rooms, a pro shop loaded with top-of-the-line equipment and gear, and great eating options where players can relish delicious cuisine while reliving their round.

For those wishing to develop their game, the club offers professional tuition from PGA-certified instructors, as well as state-of-the-art practice facilities featuring a driving range, putting green, and short game area.

Conclusion

Punta Espada Golf Club exemplifies the spirit of premium golf in the Caribbean, blending spectacular natural beauty with a tough and well built course.

Indigenous Eyes Ecological Park and Reserve

Tucked deep among the lush environment of Punta Cana, the Indigenous Eyes Ecological Park and Reserve offers a tranquil getaway from the hectic resort regions, offering visitors with an opportunity to immerse themselves in the region's natural beauty and rich biodiversity.

History and Conservation

Originally founded by the Punta Cana Ecological Foundation, the Indigenous Eyes Ecological Park and Reserve includes over 1,500 acres of protected territory, featuring virgin forests, freshwater lagoons, and various ecosystems. The park's name pays respect to the ancient Taino people who originally occupied the island, with "eyes" referring to the park's abundant freshwater springs that resemble the eyes of a sleeping animal when viewed from above.

The park is dedicated to conservation efforts aimed at maintaining the region's distinctive flora and wildlife, including endangered species such as the rhinoceros iguana and West Indian manatee. Through sustainable management techniques and educational initiatives, the park attempts to increase awareness about the importance of environmental stewardship and biodiversity protection.

Exploring the Park

Visitors to the Indigenous Eyes Ecological Park and Reserve may explore a network of well-maintained paths that run through the forest, affording possibilities for hiking, birding, and animal observation. Guided tours given by trained naturalists provide insight into the park's ecological and cultural value, allowing visitors to get a greater appreciation for the natural beauties of the Dominican Republic.

One of the features of the park is its succession of crystal-clear lagoons, fed by subterranean springs and surrounded by luxuriant flora. These hidden oasis offer a serene environment for swimming, kayaking, and leisure, giving a refreshing retreat from the heat of the Caribbean sun.

Education and Conservation Programs

The Indigenous Eyes Ecological Park and Reserve is devoted to environmental education and community engagement, offering a range of activities and projects aimed at engaging tourists and local people alike. Educational classes, guided nature walks, and volunteer opportunities give opportunity for hands-on learning and engagement in conservation activities.

Through collaborations with local schools and community groups, the park also promotes environmental awareness and sustainable practices, motivating future generations to become stewards of the natural world.

Conclusion

The Indigenous Eyes Ecological Park and Reserve serves as a tribute to the beauty and variety of the Dominican Republic, giving a haven for both wildlife and humans alike. Whether you're seeking adventure, leisure, or a deeper connection with nature, a visit to this hidden treasure in Punta Cana is guaranteed to make a lasting impact.

Hoyo Azul

Hidden within the lush vegetation of Scape Park in Cap Cana, Hoyo Azul, or "Blue Hole," is a natural wonder that captivates visitors with its gorgeous blue waters and steep limestone cliffs. This lovely cenote gives a rare opportunity to swim in the crystal-clear waters of an old sinkhole, surrounded by lush tropical flora.

Formation and Geography

Hoyo Azul was produced millions of years ago via the progressive erosion of the limestone bedrock, creating a deep cenote with wonderfully pure water. The cenote's bright blue tint is the result of sunlight passing through the water and bouncing off the limestone walls, creating an otherworldly mood that is both enchanting and memorable.

Located at the base of a high cliff, Hoyo Azul is accessible via a magnificent walking track that snakes through the forest, affording vistas of native flora and animals along the way. As visitors approach the cenote, the sound of falling water and the sight of vivid blue waters urge them to take a swim in its soothing depths.

Swimming and Adventure

Swimming at Hoyo Azul is a genuinely exciting experience, as visitors have the option to plunge into the chilly, crystal-clear waters and immerse themselves in the natural splendor of the cenote. Whether floating on the top or diving beneath the surface to investigate its underwater features, the cenote offers a cool getaway from the heat of the Caribbean sun.

For the more daring traveler, Hoyo Azul also provides options for cliff jumping and zip-lining, letting visitors to view the cenote from multiple angles. From far above, the cenote's beautiful blue waters contrast against the lush vegetation of the surrounding forest, providing a postcard-perfect sight that is great for taking stunning images and making enduring memories.

Ecological Importance

Beyond its natural beauty and recreational options, Hoyo Azul serves an important role in the local environment, acting as a supply of freshwater for native fauna and plants. The cenote's clean waters sustain a diversity of aquatic life, including tiny fish and crustaceans, while its lush surrounds provide home for a broad array of plant and animal species.

In recent years, efforts have been made to safeguard and maintain Hoyo Azul and its surrounding ecosystem, including steps to restrict tourist impact and encourage sustainable tourism practices. By promoting awareness about the need of conservation and appropriate stewardship, stakeholders strive to guarantee that this natural resource remains intact for future generations to enjoy.

Visitor Experience

Visitors to Hoyo Azul may enjoy a remarkable and engaging experience that mixes adventure, relaxation, and natural beauty. Guided excursions are provided, offering insight into the cenote's geological formation, ecological relevance, and cultural legacy. Knowledgeable guides accompany tourists down the jungle walk, pointing out native flora and animals while giving intriguing stories and anecdotes about the area's history and tradition.

Upon reaching Hoyo Azul, travelers are met by the sight of the beautiful cenote, with its sparkling blue waters set against the backdrop of towering limestone cliffs and luscious flora. Whether swimming, snorkeling, or simply soaking in the peacefulness of the surrounds, Hoyo Azul gives a unique chance to connect with nature and enjoy the beauty of the Dominican Republic's natural beauties.

Conclusion

Hoyo Azul serves as a great example of the Dominican Republic's rich natural heritage, allowing tourists a look into the beauty and diversity of the region's landscapes. From its stunning blue waters to its thick jungle environs, the cenote provides a tranquil sanctuary where visitors may escape the hustle and bustle of everyday life and immerse themselves in the beauties of the natural world.

Macao Beach

Macao Beach is a hidden treasure tucked along the northeastern coast of Punta Cana, allowing guests a calm getaway from the crowded resort districts. With its pure white beaches, crystal-clear seas, and rugged natural beauty, Macao Beach is the perfect location for sunseekers, surfers, and environment enthusiasts alike.

Natural Beauty

Macao Beach features some of the most pristine and undisturbed stretches of shoreline in Punta Cana, with its unadulterated beauty and rough appeal attracting travelers seeking a more isolated and authentic beach experience. The beach is bordered by steep cliffs and thick palm trees, giving a stunning background against the turquoise seas of the Caribbean Sea.

The beach's large length of soft, golden sands gives adequate area for sunbathing, beachcombing, and leisurely strolls along the shoreline. Whether relaxing in the shade of a swaying palm tree or having a refreshing plunge in the blue seas, visitors to Macao Beach enjoy a bit of paradise away from the throng.

Surfing and Water Sports

Macao Beach is well-known among surfers for its outstanding waves and steady swells, making it a popular destination for both new and veteran surfers. The beach's exposed location and open ocean conditions provide superb surfing conditions year-round, drawing wave riders from all over the world looking for the perfect wave.

In addition to surfing, Macao Beach provides a range of other watersports such as kiteboarding, windsurfing, and stand-up paddleboarding. Visitors who are daring may hire equipment from local sellers or join guided trips to explore the waters and feel the rush of these thrilling sports for themselves.

Local Culture and Cuisine

While Macao Beach preserves its natural and unspoiled attractiveness, it also provides insight into the Dominican culture and way of life. Visitors may mingle with friendly people who visit the beach, learn about traditional fishing techniques, and eat freshly caught seafood cooked with authentic Caribbean tastes.

Beachside eateries and vendors serve a wide range of excellent dishes, from grilled lobster and ceviche to tropical fruit smoothies and refreshing beverages. Visitors may have a leisurely seaside supper while taking in the relaxed environment and breathtaking views of the Caribbean Sea.

Conclusion

Macao Beach represents the spirit of a tropical paradise, with its clean sands, clear seas, and rugged beauty attracting people from all around. Macao Beach has something for everyone, whether you want to go on an adventure, relax, or learn about local culture. With its undisturbed natural surroundings and warm environment, it's no surprise that Macao Beach remains a must-see site for visitors to Punta Cana.

Dolphin Island Park.

Dolphin Island Park provides guests with a one-of-a-kind opportunity to engage with dolphins in their natural habitat, combining education, conservation, and lasting experiences. Located just off the coast of Punta Cana, this marine attraction lets visitors to swim, snorkel, and interact with these intelligent and lively species in a secure and regulated setting.

Interactive Dolphin Encounters

Dolphin Island Park offers a range of interactive dolphin encounters targeted to different ages and skills. Everyone may experience the beauty of interacting with these beautiful marine creatures, whether they swim with dolphins in the vast sea or have a playful encounter in shallow water.

Professional trainers and marine scientists are there to assure the safety and well-being of both tourists and dolphins, offering educational briefings and assistance during the encounter. Guests learn about dolphin behavior, anatomy, and conservation efforts to safeguard these amazing creatures and their ocean home.

Educational Programs

In addition to interactive dolphin encounters, Dolphin Island Park provides educational events and presentations to increase awareness about marine conservation and the need of maintaining ocean ecosystems. Guests may learn about dolphin biology, ecology, and the issues that marine life faces in the wild, gaining a better understanding of how humans can help preserve the health of our oceans.

Hands-on activities, guided tours, and engaging exhibits let visitors of all ages learn about the beauties of the marine environment and the vital need for conservation action. Dolphin Island Park hopes to promote care and activism for the conservation of our oceans and its inhabitants by connecting visitors with dolphins and other marine wildlife.

Conservation efforts

Dolphin Island Park is dedicated to fostering ethical and sustainable tourist activities that have minimal impact on marine habitats and species. The park follows stringent norms and regulations for animal care and welfare, ensuring that dolphins are handled with the highest dignity.

Dolphin Island Park not only provides a secure and enjoyable environment for its resident dolphins, but it also supports a number of conservation activities aimed at safeguarding maritime environments and species. Through cooperation with local and international organizations, the park contributes to research, education, and community outreach programs that help ensure the future of our seas for future generations.

Conclusion

Dolphin Island Park provides an immersive and educational experience where people may engage with dolphins in a meaningful and courteous manner.

Chapter 5

EXPLORING PUNTA CANA'S NATURAL BEAUTY.

Punta Cana, with its beautiful beaches and blue waters, is a refuge for nature lovers as well as sunbathers. From lush tropical rainforests to hidden islands and mangrove forests, the region is brimming with natural beauties waiting to be discovered.

In this chapter, we'll look at three of Punta Cana's most outstanding natural attractions: Saona Island, Los Haitises National Park, and Scape Park at Cape Cana.

Saona Island

Saona Island, off the southern coast of the Dominican Republic, is a tropical paradise known for its immaculate beaches, crystal-clear seas, and diverse marine life. This deserted island, which can only be reached by boat, provides tourists with a secluded hideaway where they may immerse themselves in nature's splendor and relax in a peaceful atmosphere.

Natural beauty.

Saona Island has some of the Caribbean's most beautiful beaches, with pristine white sands and shallow turquoise seas that reach as far as the eye can see. The island's beach, surrounded by swaying palm trees and coconut plantations, provides many chances for sunbathing, swimming, and snorkeling in the warm Caribbean Sea.

In addition to its beautiful beaches, Saona Island is home to a variety of habitats, including mangrove forests, coastal lagoons, and coral reefs. Visitors may take guided excursions through these natural areas and see a variety of local vegetation and animals, including colorful tropical fish and nesting seabirds.

Activities and Excursions

Visitors to Saona Island may enjoy a wide range of outdoor activities and excursions. Boat trips depart from Punta Cana on a regular basis, bringing passengers on beautiful cruises along the coast and over the turquoise waters of the Caribbean Sea to the island's pristine beaches.

Upon arrival, guests may engage in a range of activities such as beach volleyball, kayaking, and beachcombing. Guided snorkeling trips allow you to explore the vivid coral reefs that surround the island, while catamaran sails give a relaxing opportunity to soak up the sun and beauty.

For those looking for a more relaxed experience, lying on the beach with a cool beverage in hand is an excellent way to unwind and appreciate the natural beauty of Saona Island.

Cultural Immersion

Saona Island also allows for cultural immersion and engagement with local residents. Visitors may learn about the island's history and cultural heritage from expert guides who provide insights into the Dominicans' traditional way of life.

Local merchants and craftsmen frequently set up stalls on the beach to offer homemade goods, souvenirs, and traditional Dominican cuisine. Guests may experience local favorites like fresh seafood, tropical fruits, and coconut-based sweets while mixing with friendly people and feeling the warmth and friendliness of Dominican culture.

Conclusion

Saona Island, a tropical paradise, entices visitors with its natural beauty, beautiful beaches, and diverse marine life.

Los Haitises National Park.

Los Haitises National Park is a protected region along the Dominican Republic's northeastern coast that includes natural mangrove forests, limestone karst formations, and a network of hidden caves and caverns. This biodiverse park is home to a diverse range of flora and animals, as well as indigenous Taino petroglyphs and other archeological treasures, making it a must-see site for both nature enthusiasts and history buffs.

Natural Wonders.

Los Haitises National Park is well-known for its stunning landscapes and distinctive geological features, which have been sculpted by millions of years of erosion and tectonic action. The park's limestone karst structures rise magnificently from the surrounding woodlands, providing a stunning contrast to the turquoise waters of Samaná Bay.

Mangrove forests cover much of the park's coastline, providing critical habitat for a wide range of plant and animal species, including migratory birds, manatees, and marine reptiles. Visitors may take guided boat trips through these pristine ecosystems, marveling at the complex root systems and lush vegetation that flourish in this coastal setting.

Cave Exploration

Los Haitises National Park is known for its network of limestone caves and caverns, many of which include ancient Taino petroglyphs and pictographs. These pre-Columbian rock art monuments provide insight into the rich cultural past of the region's indigenous Taino people, who lived there for generations.

Guided cave tours take tourists through dimly lit corridors and chambers, where they may marvel at the fascinating formations and artwork on the walls. Some caverns are only accessible by boat, heightening the sense of adventure and discovery as visitors discover the park's hidden secrets.

Wildlife Watching

Los Haitises National Park is a wildlife enthusiast's paradise, with different ecosystems supporting a vast diversity of plant and animal life. Birdwatchers, in particular, will enjoy the opportunity to see rare and unique species like the Hispaniolan parrot, mangrove cuckoo, and brown pelican, which frequent the park's coastal marshes and forests.

In addition to birding, visitors may come across bats, iguanas, and freshwater turtles while exploring the park's paths and rivers. Guided nature walks and boat trips offer possibilities for animal observation and photography, allowing visitors to see these interesting species in their native environment.

Conservation and Preservation

Los Haitises National Park is dedicated to conservation and preservation activities that safeguard its distinctive ecosystems and cultural heritage. Park rangers and local guides work diligently to educate visitors on the value of responsible tourism and environmental care, so that future generations can continue to enjoy the park's natural treasures.

Through community outreach programs and collaborations with local stakeholders, the park works to promote sustainable development and ecotourism projects that benefit both the environment and the local economy. Visitors who support conservation efforts at Los Haitises National Park can help to preserve this beautiful environment for future generations.

Conclusion

Los Haitises National Park is a hidden gem waiting to be discovered, with stunning scenery, old caverns, and plentiful species that provide insight into the Dominican Republic's natural and cultural legacy.

Scape Park at Cap Cana.

Scape Park at Cap Cana is an eco-adventure park on the Dominican Republic's eastern coast that provides tourists with a thrilling choice of outdoor activities and experiences set against the region's gorgeous natural scenery. From zip-lining under the forest canopy to exploring underground caverns and cenotes, Scape Park offers thrilling activities for people of all ages.

Adventure Activities

Scape Park provides a variety of adventure activities that allow guests to experience the natural beauty and thrill of the Dominican Republic's surroundings. Zip-lining trips fly over the trees, providing stunning views of the surrounding forest and coastline, while aerial bridges and canopy walks present an exciting challenge for thrill seekers.

Scape Park provides options for cave exploring and cenote swimming in the park's underground rivers and caverns. Guided cave tours take guests through ancient limestone formations, stalactites, and stalagmites, exposing hidden chambers and underground streams created over ages of geological action.

Visitors may also cool down in the park's cenotes, which are natural sinkholes filled with crystal-clear waters and provide a welcome relief from the tropical heat. Snorkeling and swimming in these clean pools allow you to admire the underwater rock formations and witness the rich aquatic species that lives these distinct ecosystems.

Nature Trails and Explorations

Scape Park has a network of picturesque nature paths that weave through the park's thick woodlands, providing possibilities for hiking, bird viewing, and wildlife observation. Guided nature walks give information on the region's flora and animals, with trained guides pointing out local plant species and sharing intriguing facts about the park's ecosystem.

Along the pathways, visitors may see native animals like as iguanas, tropical birds, and butterflies, as well as brilliant orchids and exotic plants that flourish in the park's many ecosystems. Interpretive signage and educational exhibits give more information on the park's natural heritage and conservation initiatives, increasing the visitor experience and instilling a greater sense of environmental responsibility.

Cultural Experiences

In addition to its natural features, Scape Park provides possibilities for cultural immersion and connection with the surrounding community. Visitors may learn about the Dominican Republic's rich cultural legacy through cultural performances, traditional music, and dance displays that highlight the country's lively traditions and customs.

Local craftsmen and craftspeople frequently put up kiosks in the park to offer handcrafted souvenirs, artwork, and traditional handicrafts. Guests may explore unique products and souvenirs, supporting local craftsmen and helping to preserve Dominican culture and legacy.

Environmental Education and Conservation

Scape Park is dedicated to environmental education and conservation activities to safeguard the region's natural resources and encourage sustainable tourism practices. The park promotes biodiversity preservation, endangered species protection, and environmental stewardship via educational programs, guided tours, and informative exhibits.

To reduce its environmental impact and promote responsible tourist practices, Scape Park collaborates with local conservation groups and community partners on activities such as habitat restoration, animal monitoring, and trash management programs. By involving visitors in conservation efforts and environmental care, the park hopes to instill a feeling of responsibility and respect for the natural world.

Conclusion

Scape Park at Cap Cana provides an unparalleled combination of adventure, discovery, and cultural immersion, allowing tourists to reconnect with nature and witness the majesty of the Dominican Republic's landscapes firsthand.

Bavaro Beach

Bavaro Beach is one of Punta Cana's most renowned and popular beaches, with pure white sands, crystal-clear seas, and a dynamic environment. Bavaro Beach, located on the Dominican Republic's eastern coast, provides an idyllic location for sunbathing, swimming, water sports, and seaside leisure.

Natural beauty.

Bavaro Beach is some of Punta Cana's most beautiful scenery, with its huge expanse of smooth, golden beaches and soothing turquoise waves that reach as far as the eye can see. The beach's beautiful beachfront, fringed by swaying palm trees and lush greenery, makes an ideal setting for leisurely strolls, beachcombing, and picnics.

Bavaro Beach's calm and shallow seas make it excellent for swimming and snorkeling, with vivid coral reefs and exotic fish just a short distance from shore. Visitors may explore the underwater world at their own speed, marveling at the diverse marine life that lives in these pure coastal waters.

Water Sports and Activities

Bavaro Beach provides a diverse choice of water sports and activities for people of all ages and interests. Windsurfing, kiteboarding, and parasailing are options for adventurous vacationers, while thrill-seekers may hire jet skis or go on banana boat excursions for an amazing aquatic experience.

Beachfront loungers and umbrellas are available for rent, giving the ideal area to soak up the sun and enjoy the peaceful calm of the Caribbean Sea. Beachside pubs and restaurants serve cool drinks and delectable food, allowing travelers to sample local cuisine while enjoying spectacular ocean views.

Entertainment and Nightlife

In addition to its natural beauty and water sports, Bavaro Beach is well-known for its lively entertainment and nightlife scene. Beachfront resorts and hotels feature live music performances, dance parties, and cultural exhibits, allowing tourists to experience Dominican hospitality and nightlife.

Local vendors and craftsmen frequently put up stalls on the beach to offer handcrafted goods, souvenirs, and beachwear. Visitors may explore unique products and keepsakes while supporting local businesses and craftsmen and taking in the colorful environment of Bavaro Beach.

Conclusion

Bavaro Beach is a tropical paradise that has something for everyone, from sun-soaked leisure to adrenaline-pumping water sports and a thriving nightlife. Whether you're lazing on the sand, discovering the undersea world, or dancing the night away beneath the stars, a trip to Bavaro Beach guarantees a memorable experience in the center of Punta Cana's natural beauty.

Horseback Riding at Uvero Alto.

Horseback riding in Uvero Alto provides guests with a one-of-a-kind opportunity to discover Punta Cana's stunning landscapes and pristine beaches on horseback, creating a remarkable and immersive experience that blends adventure, relaxation, and cultural immersion.

Scenic trails and beach rides

Uvero Alto, located on the Dominican Republic's northeastern coast, with miles of gorgeous routes and isolated beaches ideal for horseback riding expeditions. Guided horseback riding trips take guests through lush tropical woods, calm farmland,

and along the Caribbean Sea's clean coasts, affording spectacular views of the region's natural wonders.

Riders may pick from a range of path alternatives, including relaxing beach rides and sunset trips, as well as more daring excursions to secret caverns and waterfalls. Whether trotting along the beach or cantering through the countryside, horseback riding in Uvero Alto is a tranquil and picturesque way to connect with nature and appreciate the beauty of Punta Cana's sceneries.

Cultural Experiences

In addition to its natural beauty, horseback riding in Uvero Alto allows for cultural immersion and engagement with the local people. Riders may visit traditional Dominican ranches and farms to learn about the region's agricultural history and participate in hands-on activities like fruit harvesting, coffee roasting, and cigar rolling.

Local guides and wranglers frequently provide stories and anecdotes about the Dominican Republic's history and culture, giving visitors insight into local customs, traditions, and ways of life. Visitors may also have the opportunity to meet and connect with friendly people while exploring the countryside and seaside communities by horseback.

Family-friendly activities.

Horseback riding in Uvero Alto is a fun family sport for riders of all ages and abilities. Many tour providers provide gentle horses and competent guides who are trained to deal with riders of all skill levels, offering a safe and pleasurable experience for everybody.

Families may bond over their love of nature and animals as they explore Punta Cana's gorgeous paths and beaches together. Children may learn important lessons about responsibility, empathy, and respect for environment by interacting with horses and experiencing the delights of outdoor adventure.

Conclusion

Horseback riding in Uvero Alto is a unique and fascinating way to see Punta Cana's natural beauty and cultural legacy. A horseback riding journey in Uvero Alto offers a memorable experience for riders of all ages and interests, whether riding along gorgeous paths, trotting along the beach, or immersing themselves in local culture.

Chapter 6

WATER ACTIVITIES IN PUNTA CANA

Punta Cana, with its crystal-clear seas and teeming marine life, is a water enthusiast's heaven. Visitors may enjoy a variety of aquatic experiences in the region, including snorkeling and diving, deep-sea fishing, and catamaran trips.

In this chapter, we'll look at three of the most popular water activities in Punta Cana: snorkeling and diving, deep-sea fishing, and catamaran and boat trips.

Snorkeling and Diving

Punta Cana has some of the Caribbean's most magnificent coral reefs and underwater habitats, making it an excellent snorkeling and diving destination. The region's crystal-clear waters, beautiful coral gardens, and rich marine life provide limitless chances for underwater exploration and discovery.

Coral reefs and Marine Life

Punta Cana's coral reefs are bursting with life, home to a diverse range of marine animals such as colorful tropical fish, sea turtles, rays, and moray eels. Snorkelers and divers may explore these underwater wonderlands, admiring the complex coral formations and seeing the intriguing behavior of the local marine life.

Popular snorkeling and diving spots in Punta Cana include the Bavaro Reef, Cocotal Reef, and the wreck of the Astron, a wrecked cargo ship that has produced an artificial reef filled with marine variety. Guided trips and excursions are provided for both novice and advanced snorkelers and divers, allowing access to some of the region's most pristine and inaccessible underwater settings.

Guided Tours and Excursions

Many tour operators in Punta Cana provide guided snorkeling and diving trips to the area's best dive locations and marine sanctuaries. Experienced guides accompany participants on underwater expeditions, giving safety briefings, equipment rentals, and skilled teaching to guarantee a fun and safe experience for everyone.

For individuals who are new to snorkeling or diving, beginning training and certification programs are available, allowing them to master the fundamentals of underwater exploration while also earning recognized diving credentials. Experienced divers may go on advanced dives to explore deeper reefs, underwater caverns, and offshore shipwrecks, while photographers and videographers can take breathtaking photographs of the region's diverse marine life.

Conservation and Environmental Awareness.

Punta Cana is dedicated to preserving its coral reefs and marine habitats via conservation efforts and environmental awareness campaigns. Tour operators and dive shops encourage appropriate diving methods such as avoiding contact with delicate coral formations, using buoyancy control, and reducing underwater disruptions to marine life.

Punta Cana not only promotes sustainable tourist practices, but it also supports marine conservation programs such as coral reef preservation and restoration, water quality monitoring, and the protection of endangered species. By promoting awareness about the importance of coral reef protection and encouraging active engagement in marine stewardship activities, Punta Cana hopes to safeguard the long-term health and vibrancy of its underwater ecosystems for future generations to enjoy.

Conclusion

Snorkeling and diving at Punta Cana provide a fascinating peek into the beauty and diversity of the Caribbean's underwater ecosystem. A snorkeling or diving expedition in Punta Cana offers an exciting journey for water enthusiasts of all ages and skill levels, whether they are exploring vivid coral reefs, experiencing colorful marine life, or learning about the region's conservation initiatives.

Deep Sea Fishing

Deep-sea fishing is a popular leisure activity in Punta Cana, where fishermen may pit their abilities against some of the world's most valuable game species in the turquoise seas of the Caribbean Sea. With its wealth of offshore fishing areas, various marine environments, and competent charter captains, Punta Cana is regarded as one of the Caribbean's best fishing locations.

Gamefish Species

Punta Cana's deep-sea fishing areas are home to a diverse range of game fish species, including marlin, sailfish, dorado (mahimahi), wahoo, tuna, and barracuda. Anglers may target these valuable game fish all year, with peak fishing seasons varied according to species and ocean conditions.

Marlin, including blue marlin, white marlin, and sailfish, are among the most popular game fish in Punta Cana, with options for both trolling and live bait fishing. These huge pelagic predators present a thrilling challenge for experienced fishermen, frequently putting up a hard battle and testing the boundaries of fisherman skill and tenacity.

Fishing Charters and Guides

Numerous charter companies in Punta Cana provide deep-sea fishing trips for fishermen of all skill levels, with fully equipped boats, competent captains, and informed staff to ensure a successful and pleasurable fishing trip. Charter boats come in a variety of sizes, from little skiffs and center consoles to big sport fishing yachts, serving parties of various sizes and budgets.

Experienced captains and crew members are knowledgeable with the local fishing areas and may offer helpful advice on fishing tactics, equipment selection, and seasonal fishing trends. Whether trolling offshore for billfish or bottom fishing for reef species, anglers can rely on their guides to increase their chances of landing a monster catch.

Tournaments and Events

Punta Cana holds a number of notable fishing contests and events throughout the year, bringing fishermen from all over the world to compete for cash prizes and bragging rights. These contests celebrate the region's historic fishing legacy while also benefiting the local economy by encouraging tourism and conservation initiatives.

The International Billfish Shootout, Blue Marlin Tournament, and White Marlin Tournament are among the most anticipated events on the Punta Cana fishing calendar, attracting elite fishermen and teams to participate in a pleasant but competitive environment. Aside from the thrill of the pursuit, participants may enjoy social events, awards ceremonies, and camaraderie with other fishermen as they relate their stories of the one that got away.

Conservation and Sustainability

Punta Cana is dedicated to supporting sustainable fishing techniques and marine conservation measures that will maintain the long-term health and sustainability of its marine ecosystems. Charter operators and fishing guides follow catch-and-release regulations for some species, including as billfish and sharks, to reduce the impact on fragile populations and ensure the survival of recreational fishing in the region.

In addition to catch-and-release methods, Punta Cana promotes scientific research and conservation efforts targeted at analyzing fish populations, monitoring habitat health, and safeguarding vital marine environments. Punta Cana aims to maintain its unique fishing history for future generations by encouraging safe fishing techniques and environmental management.

Conclusion

Deep-sea fishing in Punta Cana allows anglers to experience the thrill of the chase as well as the excitement of landing trophy-sized game fish in one of the Caribbean's most popular fishing spots.

Catamaran and Boat Tours.

Catamaran and boat trips are popular ways to explore Punta Cana's magnificent shoreline and pure waterways, providing guests with a relaxing and scenic opportunity to enjoy the beauty of the Caribbean Sea. Sunset cruises and snorkeling expeditions, as well as island-hopping excursions and party boats, are available to suit any taste or budget.

Island-hopping Excursions

The island-hopping adventure is a popular catamaran and boat cruise in Punta Cana, allowing guests to explore neighboring islands, cays, and quiet beaches. These cruises normally leave from Punta Cana and travel to scenic locations such as Saona Island, Catalina Island, and Isla Catalinita, among others.

Guests on the island-hopping adventure may enjoy sailing around the coastline on a spacious catamaran or luxury yacht, taking in panoramic views of the Caribbean Sea and neighboring surroundings. Along the route, the boat may stop at numerous snorkeling areas, where visitors may put on masks and fins and explore bright coral reefs and swim among tropical fish in the warm, clear seas.

Once onshore, tourists may relax on gorgeous beaches, wander along the shoreline, and soak up the sun while the tour organizers supply cool beverages and refreshments. Some trips may also include beachfront barbecues, beach activities, and cultural performances, providing an entire day of fun and relaxation in paradise.

Sunset Cruises

Sunset cruises are another popular option for catamaran and boat trips in Punta Cana, since they provide a romantic and memorable way to conclude the day. Guests can set sail in the late afternoon or early evening for a leisurely cruise down the coast as the sun sets below the horizon, painting the sky with a beautiful display of hues.

As the boat glides over the calm seas, passengers may unwind on deck with a glass of champagne or a tropical drink while admiring the tranquillity and beauty of the Caribbean sunset. Live music, entertainment, and onboard amenities like unlimited drinks and hors d'oeuvres round out the experience, resulting in a wonderful evening of romance and leisure on the sea.

Snorkelling Adventures

Snorkeling activities are a great way to combine sightseeing and underwater exploration on catamaran and boat trips in Punta Cana. These trips generally include stops at popular snorkeling spots, where passengers may put on their snorkel gear and plunge into the crystal-clear waters to see beautiful coral reefs, tropical fish, and other marine life.

Guided snorkeling trips include insightful commentary and safety advice to keep tourists comfortable and confident as they explore the underwater world. Knowledgeable guides may point out unusual marine animals, discuss the importance of coral reef protection, and provide advice for finding hidden riches beneath the seas.

Party Boats

For those looking for a more lively ambiance and a taste of Caribbean nightlife, party boats are a popular option for catamaran and boat trips in Punta Cana. These high-energy trips usually include onboard DJs, live music, dancing, and a festive mood, resulting in a vibrant party scene on the water.

Guests may dance the day away on deck, sip cool cocktails from the onboard bar, and socialize with other revelers as they sail around the coast. Some party boat trips may also make stops at beach clubs, floating bars, or private islands, where visitors may continue the fun with beach games, water sports, and beachfront entertainment.

Conclusion

Catamaran and boat trips are a fun and unique way to discover Punta Cana's natural beauty and stunning landscapes, offering guests options for relaxation, adventure, and cultural immersion while on the water. A catamaran or boat excursion in Punta Cana offers a memorable experience for tourists of all ages and interests, whether they are island hopping, snorkeling, taking a sunset cruise, or partying the day away.

Parasailing and Jetskiing

Parasailing and jet skiing are two thrilling water activities that allow guests to feel the rush of speed and adventure while admiring the stunning vistas of Punta Cana's shoreline and blue ocean. Whether flying far above the water or racing over the waves, these thrilling activities provide an amazing way to discover the beauty of the Caribbean.

Parasailing

Parasailing, also known as parascending or parakiting, is an exciting water activity that combines the exhilaration of flying with the serenity of floating above the ocean. Participants are tied to a parachute-like canopy, which is then connected to a speedboat by a tow line. As the boat speeds up, the parachute fills with air, propelling the rider into the sky for a bird's-eye view of the shoreline and surrounding scenery.

Parasailing businesses in Punta Cana offer tandem flights, which allow two riders to soar together while locked in a shared harness. This shared experience heightens the exhilaration and camaraderie as players alternate between feeling weightless and free and taking in panoramic views of the ocean and shoreline.

Parasailing flights normally last 10 to 15 minutes, allowing riders to relax and enjoy the sense of soaring, with the wind in their hair and the sun warming their skin. Some operators may provide longer flights or other services, such as picture or video packages, to help passengers remember this amazing experience.

Jet Skiing

Jet skiing is another popular water sport in Punta Cana, where riders can race across the waves at great speeds while exploring the shoreline and nearby islands. Jet skis, also known as personal watercraft (PWC), are tiny, powered watercraft that are simple to navigate and operate, making them suitable for riders of all skill levels.

Jet ski rentals in Punta Cana are accessible at a variety of coastal spots and resorts, allowing riders to explore the coastline at their own speed. Guided jet ski trips are also offered, with professional instructors providing safety instructions, navigation suggestions, and local information.

Jet ski trips may include stops at gorgeous landmarks, isolated beaches, and natural wonders, allowing riders to uncover hidden treasures and shoot breathtaking images of their experience. Riders may either cruise at a leisurely speed, taking in the sun and surroundings, or rev up the throttle and enjoy the adrenaline rush as they zoom across the waves.

Safety and Regulations

Parasailing and jet skiing providers in Punta Cana prioritize safety, with strong laws and procedures in place to safeguard participants and the maritime environment. Before each activity begins, operators give all participants a safety lecture, an equipment check, and advice on basic riding methods.

Participants must wear personal flotation devices (PFDs) or life jackets when parasailing or jet skiing, and operators may set age and weight limits for safety concerns. Riders are also asked to observe basic safety rules, including as keeping a safe distance from other boats, adhering to speed restrictions, and avoiding irresponsible conduct.

By following safety rules and laws, parasailing and jet skiing companies in Punta Cana seek to give participants with safe and fun experiences while conserving the maritime environment's natural beauty and purity.

Conclusion

Parasailing and jet skiing are exhilarating ways to enjoy the beauty and excitement of Punta Cana's shoreline, offering riders adrenaline-pumping experiences and spectacular vistas of the Caribbean Sea.

Kiteboarding and Windsurfing.

Kiteboarding and windsurfing are two popular water sports in Punta Cana, where fans may use the strength of the wind and waves to glide over the ocean with speed and agility. Punta Cana's steady trade winds, warm waters, and wide-open beaches make it a great location for these exciting activities all year long.

Kiteboarding

Kiteboarding, often known as kitesurfing, is an exciting water activity that combines aspects of surfing, wakeboarding, and paragliding. Participants harness the force of the wind by flying a giant kite and pushing themselves over the water on a board while doing acrobatics and maneuvers.

Kiteboarders at Punta Cana may experience world-class kiteboarding conditions because to the region's constant trade winds and shallow, sandy-bottomed beaches. Along the shore, there are several kiteboarding schools and rental businesses where novices may learn from licensed instructors while experienced riders can rent equipment and attack the waves.

Kiteboarding destinations such as Playa Blanca, Kite Beach, and Macao Beach provide plenty of room for riders to launch and land their kites, as well as flat sea and rolling waves for practicing tricks and jumps. Downwind trips and guided tours are also offered, allowing riders to explore several kiteboarding locations and determine the optimum circumstances for their ability level.

Windsurfing

Windsurfing is another popular water sport in Punta Cana, with a unique combination of sailing and surfing that tests both the body and the mind. Participants utilize a board with a sail tied to a mast to harness the force of the wind, allowing them to glide across the water while performing a variety of moves and acrobatics.

Windsurfers at Punta Cana may enjoy a variety of conditions, including flat water lagoons, rolling waves, and offshore swells. Windsurfing schools and rental businesses provide beginner instruction from licensed instructors, teaching the fundamentals of board control, sail management, and wind awareness in a safe and friendly atmosphere.

Experienced windsurfers may test their talents at the region's numerous windsurfing areas, such as Playa Blanca, Macao Beach, and Bavaro Beach, against demanding wind and wave conditions. Punta Cana also hosts monthly windsurfing tournaments and events, inviting professional riders and fans from all over the world to exhibit their skills and compete for awards.

Equipment Rental and Lessons

Windsurfing and kiteboarding equipment may be rented from beachside resorts, water sports facilities, and specialist stores all across Punta Cana. Rental packages often include boards, sails, harnesses, and safety equipment, allowing riders to get out on the lake with everything they need for a day of fun.

Beginners should take lessons from licensed instructors to acquire appropriate skills, safety measures, and water etiquette. Lessons are provided for all ability levels, from complete beginners to skilled riders eager to learn new tricks and maneuvers. With individualized teaching and hands-on direction, participants may advance fast and confidently in their chosen water activity.

Safety and Considerations.

Kiteboarding and windsurfing need strict adherence to safety requirements and safeguards. This involves inspecting equipment for damage or wear, using proper safety gear such as helmets and life jackets, and staying vigilant of weather and water risks.

Riders must respect the rights of other beachgoers and water users while also following local water sports legislation and standards. Participants may contribute to a safe and pleasurable time on the lake by exercising excellent sportsmanship and environmental care.

Environmental Awareness

Punta Cana is devoted to environmental sustainability and responsible tourist practices, which include water sports like kiteboarding and windsurfing. Participants are advised to reduce their influence on the marine environment by avoiding contact with coral reefs and vulnerable ecosystems, appropriately disposing of garbage, and respecting marine life and animals.

Local organizations and conservation groups aim to safeguard and maintain Punta Cana's coastal habitats, which include coral reefs, mangrove forests, and marine sanctuaries. Participants may help the region's natural resources remain healthy and sustainable by supporting these initiatives and engaging in responsible water sports.

Conclusion

Kiteboarding and windsurfing are exciting ways to experience the wind and waves of Punta Cana's shoreline, offering riders with an adrenaline rush and a deep connection to nature.

Chapter 7

CULTURAL EXPERIENCES IN PUNTA CANA.

Punta Cana is recognized for more than just its beautiful beaches and exciting water sports; it also has a rich cultural past and strong local traditions.

In this chapter, we will look at three immersive cultural activities that allow tourists to get closer to the heart and soul of Punta Cana: visiting indigenous communities, exploring local art and artisan markets, and taking Dominican cuisine cooking courses.

Visit Indigenous Villages

A tour to indigenous communities is one of the most interesting cultural experiences in Punta Cana, as it allows guests to learn about the region's indigenous peoples' customs, traditions, and way of life. These villages offer visitors a fascinating glimpse into the history and heritage of the Dominican Republic's indigenous Taino culture, allowing them to interact with locals, participate in traditional activities, and learn about the challenges and opportunities that indigenous communities face today.

Cultural Immersion

Visiting an indigenous hamlet allows guests to immerse themselves in the bright sights, sounds, and flavors of Taino culture, as well as experience traditional music, dance, and storytelling first hand. Local guides and community members frequently offer guided tours and demonstrations, telling information about the Taino people's history and customs while also providing insight into their long-lasting impact on Dominican culture.

Visitors may be able to engage in cultural activities like as pottery making, basket weaving, and traditional cuisine, which teach ancient techniques and skills passed down through generations. Visitors can acquire a better understanding of Taino culture's craftsmanship and creative expression by conversing with local artisans and craftspeople.

Environmental Education

In addition to cultural immersion, trips to indigenous villages frequently involve opportunity to learn about the value of environmental protection and sustainable living practices in indigenous communities. Many villages are located in environmentally fragile environments, such as rainforests, mountains, or coastal regions, where inhabitants rely on natural resources for a living and cultural identity.

Guided nature walks, botanical excursions, and ecological seminars teach visitors about indigenous populations' traditional knowledge and methods for protecting and preserving their natural environment. Visitors visiting indigenous cultures can learn about the complex interaction between humans and the environment through medicinal plants and herbal treatments, as well as sustainable agricultural practices and biodiversity protection.

Cultural Exchange and Support.

Visiting indigenous villages in Punta Cana allows people to participate in meaningful cultural interaction while also supporting local communities via responsible tourism practices. Many villages invite visitors as a way to share their heritage and customs with the rest of the world while also providing revenue and economic possibilities for local residents.

By purchasing handcrafted crafts, artwork, and locally manufactured commodities, visitors may directly support indigenous artists and businesses, helping to preserve traditional crafts and cultural traditions. Furthermore, revenues from tours and cultural events are frequently directed toward community development projects, educational initiatives, and conservation efforts that benefit the whole community.

Conclusion

A tour to an indigenous hamlet in Punta Cana offers a unique and important chance to interact with the Dominican Republic's rich cultural history while also learning about the Taino people's traditions, rituals, and way of life. Visitors may help to preserve and celebrate indigenous culture by engaging in cultural immersion, environmental education, and responsible tourism activities that benefit the well-being and prosperity of local communities.

Local Arts and Crafts Markets

Exploring local art and craft markets is a delightful way to experience Punta Cana's vibrant creativity and cultural diversity, showcasing the talents of local artisans and craftsmen while also providing visitors with a unique opportunity to purchase handmade souvenirs, artwork, and gifts to commemorate their trip.

Artisanal crafts and handmade goods

Punta Cana's art and craft markets are bursting with a colorful array of artisanal crafts and handcrafted items, ranging from traditional handicrafts and folk art to modern designs and imaginative ideas. Visitors may peruse a wide range of things, including handcrafted jewelry, ceramics, textiles, wood carvings, paintings, and sculptures, all created with skill and care by local craftsmen.

Many craftsmen are inspired by the Dominican Republic's natural beauty and cultural legacy, infusing themes like tropical patterns, indigenous symbols, and brilliant colors into their works. Visitors may find one-of-a-kind artworks that capture the passion and uniqueness of Punta Cana, making for memorable and significant vacation gifts.

Cultural Exchange and Interaction.

Exploring local art and craft fairs allows tourists to exchange cultural ideas and connect with local artisans and craftspeople. Many markets provide live demonstrations and workshops where visitors may observe craftsmen at work, learn about ancient techniques and materials, and even try their hand at producing their own masterpieces with the help of professional teachers.

Interacting with artists helps visitors to obtain an understanding of the creative process, hear tales about the motivation behind their work, and learn about the cultural value of various craft traditions. Whether conversing with a potter, observing a weaver at the loom, or appreciating a painter's brushstrokes, tourists may engage with the brilliant people who bring Punta Cana's cultural legacy to life.

Supporting local artisans

Visitors who buy handcrafted goods and artwork directly from local craftsmen at art and craft fairs may help to promote the livelihoods and economic development of creative people and communities. Unlike mass-produced souvenirs, handcrafted objects provide a distinct feeling of authenticity and workmanship, reflecting the craftsmen' time, talent, and passion to producing each piece.

Shopping at art and craft fairs not only benefits local craftsmen, but it also helps to preserve and promote traditional craft practices and cultural heritage. Many craftsmen rely on traditional methods and materials passed down through generations, ensuring that ancient craft traditions persist and grow in the modern world.

Conclusion

Exploring local art and craft markets in Punta Cana takes guests on a compelling trip through the heart of Dominican creativity and cultural expression, giving possibilities for discovery, inspiration, and interaction with local artisans and craftsmen.

Dominican Cuisine Cooking Classes.

Dominican cuisine is a wonderful combination of African, European, and indigenous flavors that represent the Dominican Republic's broad cultural background and culinary traditions. Taking a cooking class in Punta Cana is an excellent opportunity to immerse yourself in the region's rich culinary culture, learning how to produce traditional Dominican meals while also learning about the ingredients, methods, and cultural importance of each recipe.

Experiential learning

Dominican cuisine cooking workshops provide hands-on learning experiences in which participants may roll up their sleeves, put on aprons, and start cooking alongside professional teachers. Whether newbie chefs or seasoned foodies, participants of all skill levels can benefit from the opportunity to learn new recipes, methods, and culinary ideas in a fun and friendly setting.

Classes often begin with an introduction to Dominican cuisine, focusing on important ingredients, taste profiles, and cooking methods that are central to the Dominican Republic's culinary heritage. Participants may next begin creating a variety of classic recipes, such as mangu (mashed plantains), sancocho (hearty stew), or tostones (fried plantains), with the teacher providing step-by-step directions and demonstrations.

Local Ingredients and Flavors

Dominican cuisine cooking schools frequently stress the use of fresh, locally obtained products, which are plentiful in Punta Cana's tropical environment. Participants may get the chance to visit local markets or farms to choose items such as tropical fruits, root vegetables, herbs, and spices, developing an understanding of the vivid tastes and fragrances that distinguish Dominican cuisine.

Instructors may give stories and anecdotes on the cultural importance of certain ingredients, as well as suggestions for selecting, storing, and preparing them to improve flavor and texture in recipes. Participants may anticipate to work with a wide range of foods, including essentials like rice, beans, yuca, and plantains, as well as fish, poultry, and meats popular in Dominican cuisine.

Traditional Recipes and Techniques

Culinary workshops in Punta Cana teach traditional Dominican recipes and culinary skills that have been passed down through generations. Participants are taught how to create foods using genuine methods and materials, such as a mortar and pestle for grinding spices, a wooden pilón for mashing plantains, and traditional cooking containers including calderos (cast-iron pots) and cazuelas.

Instructors offer step-by-step instructions and hands-on experience, showing correct techniques for chopping, seasoning, marinating, and cooking ingredients to produce the best flavor and texture in each meal. Participants may ask questions, seek clarification, and receive tailored feedback as they go through each dish, allowing them to acquire confidence and mastery in their culinary talents.

Cultural insights and traditions

Cooking lessons in Punta Cana are more than simply a culinary adventure; they also provide vital insights into Dominican culture, history, and traditions. Instructors may tell students about the origins of particular recipes, the impact of diverse cultural groups on Dominican cuisine, and the importance of food in social gatherings, festivities, and everyday life.

Participants may also learn about Dominican dining customs and etiquette, such as the value of sharing meals with family and friends, being welcoming to guests, and enjoying each bite with thanks and respect. Cooking and eating meals together allows participants to form friendships, enhance cultural understanding, and create lasting memories of their stay in Punta Cana.

Tasting and Sharing

One of the attractions of Dominican cuisine cooking lessons is the chance to taste and appreciate the results of your efforts at the conclusion of the session. Participants gather around the table to enjoy the meals they have made, exchanging tales, laughter, and friendship while indulging in a delectable feast of typical Dominican cuisine.

Instructors may give extra information on taste profiles, ingredient combinations, and serving suggestions, encouraging participants to try their own changes and interpretations of the recipes. Participants leave the workshop feeling inspired and motivated to reproduce the meals at home, sharing the flavors of Punta Cana's culinary legacy with family and friends all over the world.

Conclusion

Dominican cuisine cooking lessons are a fun and savory way to immerse yourself in Punta Cana's culinary traditions, teaching you how to make genuine meals with fresh, locally obtained ingredients and traditional cooking methods.

Merengue and Bachata Dance Lessons.

Merengue and Bachata are two prominent dance forms with strong roots in Dominican culture. Dance lessons in Punta Cana allow guests to learn these vivid and rhythmic dances from professional instructors, immersing them in the music, movement, and spirit of Dominican dance culture.

Merengue Dance Lessons.

Merengue is the Dominican Republic's national dance, distinguished by its upbeat speed, addictive rhythm, and fun hip motions. Merengue began in rural towns and villages and has grown over generations into a treasured cultural heritage embraced at festivals, celebrations, and social events across the country.

Merengue dance classes in Punta Cana normally begin with an overview of the dance's history and origins, emphasizing its African and European influences, as well as its position in Dominican society. Participants learn fundamental steps, turns, and footwork patterns, progressively increasing their confidence and ability as they practice with partners and groups.

Experienced teachers give customized coaching and criticism, assisting participants in developing perfect posture, timing, and style so that they may express themselves genuinely through movement. Participants of all skill levels may benefit from learning Merengue in a pleasant and friendly setting full of laughter, friendship, and rhythm.

Bachata Dance Lessons

Bachata is another popular dance form in the Dominican Republic, distinguished by its romantic songs, sensuous motions, and close partner connection. Bachata originated in the Dominican Republic's rural areas and has since grown into a global phenomenon, enjoyed by dancers and aficionados all over the world.

Bachata dancing classes in Punta Cana emphasize the fundamental steps, twists, and body motions that define this passionate and expressive dance form. Participants learn how to connect with their partner using subtle clues, body language, and musical interpretation, resulting in a joyful and fluid dancing relationship on the floor.

Instructors lead participants through a series of planned sequences and improvised activities to help them gain confidence, creativity, and connection in their dance. Participants may expect to master conventional Bachata steps including the basic, side step, and forward-and-back, as well as more advanced motions and styling methods to help them expand their dance repertoire.

Cultural Awareness and Music Appreciation

Merengue and Bachata dance courses teach more than simply dancing technique; they also provide significant insights into Dominican culture, music, and social norms. Instructors may tell anecdotes about the history and evolution of Merengue and Bachata, emphasizing the dances' cultural relevance in Dominican society.

Participants learn to understand the rhythmic intricacy and emotional depth of Merengue and Bachata music by identifying the unique instruments, rhythms, and melodies that define each style. Understanding the cultural backdrop and musical intricacies helps participants appreciate the dances and connect more intimately with the music and movement.

Social Dance and Celebration

Merengue and Bachata dance courses frequently conclude with social dancing sessions in which participants may put their newly learned abilities to use in a fun and encouraging environment. Whether dancing with partners or in group dances, participants may experience the excitement of dancing to live music or recorded tracks while surrounded by other dance lovers who share their enthusiasm.

Social dancing allows individuals to experience the joy and camaraderie of Dominican dance culture firsthand, forming bonds with others through shared movement and expression. Whether dancing under the stars at a beachside party or in a frenetic dance club, Merengue and Bachata may be celebrated with flair, grace, and excitement.

Conclusion

Merengue and Bachata dance courses in Punta Cana provide an immersive and exciting cultural experience in which participants may learn traditional Dominican dances while connecting with the bright rhythms and spirit of the Caribbean.

Cigar Rolling Workshops.

Cigar rolling seminars in Punta Cana provide tourists with a unique chance to learn about the art and craft of cigar creation from professional torcedores (cigar rollers), as well as receive insight into the traditions, practices, and culture surrounding this renowned Dominican activity.

History and Heritage of Cigar Making

Cigar rolling classes often begin with an overview of the Dominican Republic's cigar manufacturing history and legacy, emphasizing the country's rich tobacco-growing traditions and reputation as one of the world's leading cigar-producing countries. Participants learn about the many tobacco kinds used in the Dominican Republic, how they are grown and harvested, and how professional blenders work to create unique cigar mixes.

Instructors may provide stories and anecdotes on the cultural significance of cigars in Dominican society, such as their use in social events, festivals, and rituals. Participants get a greater understanding for the workmanship and creativity involved in cigar creation, as well as the cultural legacy and economic significance of the Dominican cigar industry.

Hands-on Cigar Rolling

During cigar rolling courses, participants may roll their own cigars with the help of skilled torcedores who show proper procedures and offer step-by-step instructions throughout the process. Participants will learn how to pick and prepare tobacco leaves, roll and shape the filler, binder, and wrapper, and finish the cigar with a classic cap and label.

Rolling a cigar by hand involves accuracy, patience, and attention to detail as participants strive to make a cigar that is properly formed and neatly wrapped, resulting in a delightful smoking experience. Instructors provide customized comments and advice, assisting participants in troubleshooting any issues and refining their rolling technique to make high-quality cigars.

Cigar Taste and Appreciation

After the cigars are rolled, attendees may enjoy the results of their labor during a cigar tasting session, where they can sample a variety of excellent Dominican cigars and evaluate mixes, sizes, and flavors. Instructors teach students how to correctly cut, light, and smoke a cigar, as well as how to detect subtle differences in flavor, fragrance, and structure.

Cigar tasting workshops allow attendees to discover the numerous tastes and qualities that set Dominican cigars apart, from the rich, earthy notes of Maduro wrappers to the spicy, peppery aromas of Corojo tobacco. Participants can share their experiences and insights with other cigar fans, encouraging conversation and fellowship.

Cultural Exchange and Connection.

Cigar rolling workshops give more than simply education in cigar creation; they also allow for cultural interaction and engagement with local craftsmen and cigar enthusiasts. Participants can learn from seasoned torcedores who have dedicated their lives to mastering the art of cigar rolling, acquiring knowledge of their techniques, traditions, and personal experiences in the tobacco industry.

Visitors can form deep relationships and friendships with local cigar producers and fellow participants via a common enthusiasm for cigars and cigar culture. Participants can interact with individuals who share their interest in cigars and Dominican culture by trading tales, offering suggestions, or simply enjoying a smoke together.

Cigar rolling courses in Punta Cana provide an immersive and stimulating cultural experience, allowing participants to immerse themselves in the intriguing world of cigar production while learning about the history, legacy, and artistry of the Dominican cigar industry. Participants may get a remarkable and authentic peek into the art and culture of Dominican cigars by rolling their own cigars, tasting quality blends, or conversing with other lovers.

Finally, Punta Cana provides a varied range of cultural activities, allowing tourists to immerse themselves in the Dominican Republic's colorful traditions, legacy, and creativity. There are several ways to interact with Punta Cana's rich cultural tapestry, including visiting indigenous communities and exploring local art markets, as well as learning traditional dances, preparing Dominican cuisine, and making cigars.

Chapter 8

SHOPPING AT PUNTA CANA

Visitors to Punta Cana may enjoy a wide range of shopping opportunities, from luxury boutiques and designer stores to local markets and artisanal businesses. Punta Cana provides everything for everyone, including souvenirs, clothes, jewelry, and one-of-a-kind handcrafted crafts.

In this chapter, we will look at three of Punta Cana's best shopping destinations: Punta Cana Village, Palma Real Shopping Village, and Plaza Bavaro.

Punta Cana Village

Punta Cana Village is a lovely retail and entertainment center in the heart of Punta Cana, with a variety of upmarket boutiques, specialized stores, restaurants, and entertainment venues. Punta Cana hamlet, designed in the form of a European hamlet, is a popular destination for both travelers and residents, offering a peaceful and pleasant environment for shopping, dining, and leisure activities.

Shopping

Punta Cana Village has a range of stores and boutiques where guests may purchase designer apparel and accessories, as well as unusual presents and souvenirs. Fashion fans will like the collection of fashionable stores that provide the most recent fashions in clothes, footwear, and accessories from both local and international designers.

Art enthusiasts will enjoy perusing the galleries and artisan stores, which showcase a varied selection of artwork, including paintings, sculptures, ceramics, and handcrafted jewelry created by brilliant local artisans. Visitors may find unique works that encapsulate the beauty and character of the Dominican Republic, making for memorable and significant travel keepsakes.

Dining and Entertainment

In addition to shopping, Punta Cana Village has a diverse range of dining options, from informal cafés and bistros to upmarket restaurants and gourmet diners. Visitors may sample a variety of different cuisines, including Italian, French, Mexican, and Caribbean dishes, as well as fresh seafood, grilled meats, and regional delicacies.

After a day of shopping and dining, guests may unwind at one of the village's entertainment venues, which may feature live music performances, cultural activities, or outdoor festivals.

Services and Amenities

Punta Cana Village also offers a variety of services and amenities to help guests enjoy their shopping and leisure experiences. Banks, pharmacies, supermarkets, beauty salons, and spas are examples of such establishments, as are parks, playgrounds, and fitness centers.

Visitors may benefit from handy services such as currency exchange, ATM machines, and concierge assistance with travel plans, bookings, and local suggestions. With plenty of parking, wheelchair accessible, and a pleasant and inviting ambiance, Punta Cana Village seeks to provide a comfortable and easy shopping experience for people of all ages and interests.

Conclusion

Punta Cana Village provides a beautiful combination of shopping, eating, and entertainment in a gorgeous village environment, giving guests a one-of-a-kind and entertaining shopping experience in the center of Punta Cana. Visitors to this delightful shopping location may uncover a world of discoveries and joys, whether they explore the shops and galleries, eat exquisite cuisine, or simply take in the atmosphere.

Palma Real Shopping Village.

Palma Real Shopping Village is a prominent shopping and entertainment area in Bavaro, just a few minutes from Punta Cana's beaches. Palma Real, with its open-air design, rich landscaping, and magnificent architecture, provides a sophisticated and upmarket retail experience set in a tropical paradise.

Luxury shopping

Palma Real features a carefully picked assortment of premium shops and upmarket retailers that provide designer apparel, accessories, jewelry, and lifestyle items. Fashionistas will enjoy perusing the latest collections from recognized brands such as Ralph Lauren, Armani Exchange, Tommy Hilfiger, and Lacoste, as well as special stores featuring local andinternational designers.

In addition to fashion, Palma Real has specialist businesses that sell everything from fine jewelry and watches to leather products, cosmetics, and home décor. Visitors may embark on a shopping spree and find a variety of high-end goods and luxury things to fit their likes and preferences.

Dining and Entertainment

Palma Real has a broad assortment of dining alternatives, including restaurants, cafés, and diners providing exquisite food from across the world. Whether you're hungry Italian spaghetti, Japanese sushi, American burgers, or Caribbean seafood, Palma Real has something to satisfy you.

After dinner, tourists may unwind at one of Palma Real's entertainment options, which may include movie theaters, pubs, nightclubs, or live music venues. Palma Real provides a dynamic and energetic atmosphere for tourists to enjoy, whether they are watching a blockbuster movie, having a drink with friends, or dancing the night away to live music.

Events and Activities

Palma Real organizes a wide range of events and activities throughout the year, including fashion shows, cultural festivals, live concerts, and art exhibitions. Visitors may check the event calendar to see what's occurring during their stay and take advantage of special deals, discounts, or entertainment options.

Palma Real also provides facilities like as free Wi-Fi, valet parking, and concierge services to help tourists enjoy their shopping and leisure experiences. Palma Real retail Village, with its accessible location, exquisite ambiance, and world-class retail and eating options, is a must-see for discriminating shoppers and luxury aficionados in Punta Cana.

Conclusion

Palma Real Shopping Village provides guests with a sophisticated and upmarket shopping experience in the center of Bavaro, as well as a beautiful and trendy location for eating and entertainment. Visitors to Palma Real Shopping Village may have a wonderful and exquisite shopping experience, whether they are on a shopping spree, relishing gourmet cuisine, or simply soaking in the environment.

Plaza Bavaro.

Plaza Bavaro is a lively commercial mall in the middle of Bavaro, not far from Punta Cana's resort sector. Plaza Bavaro, with its bustling ambiance, wide mix of retailers, and energetic entertainment choices, provides travelers with a convenient and entertaining shopping experience with a local twist.

Local shops and boutiques.

Plaza Bavaro is home to a diverse collection of stores and boutiques selling anything from apparel and accessories to souvenirs and presents. Visitors may visit local artisan stores and craft booths to find handcrafted jewelry, ceramics, artwork, and other unique things created by brilliant Dominican craftsmen.

Plaza Bavaro also sells clothing, footwear, swimwear, and accessories for men, women, and children. Visitors may peruse the newest designs and trends, as well as traditional styles and beachwear suitable for a day at the beach.

Souvenirs and Keepsakes

Plaza Bavaro has a number of souvenir shops and gift stores where tourists may discover a variety of memories and keepsakes. From t-shirts and caps to keychains, magnets, and handcrafted souvenirs, there is something for everyone's taste and budget.

Visitors may purchase souvenirs showcasing Punta Cana's characteristic emblems, such as palm trees, seashells, and tropical patterns, as well as designs inspired by the Dominican Republic's rich history and tradition. Whether buying for friends, family, or themselves, Plaza Bavaro offers the ideal souvenir of their vacation in paradise.

Dining and Entertainment

Plaza Bavaro has a range of eating alternatives, including restaurants, cafés, and diners providing great food from across the world. Visitors can dine slowly or quickly before continuing their shopping activities.

Plaza Bavaro offers a variety of entertainment alternatives, including movie theaters, arcades, and live music venues, where guests may rest after a long day of shopping. Plaza Bavaro has something for everyone, whether you want to watch the newest blockbuster movie, play arcade games with pals, or dance to live music beneath the stars.

Local Flavors and Delights.

Plaza Bavaro's colorful food court is a must-see for visitors, offering a wide range of local specialties, street food, and foreign cuisine. Mofongo, empanadas, and tostones are native Dominican dishes, but pizza, sushi, and burgers are global favorites.

Visitors may savor traditional tastes and regional delicacies while also trying innovative meals and culinary innovations inspired by the Dominican Republic's many cultures and cuisines. Plaza Bavaro's food court is a favorite meeting location for both residents and visitors, because to its relaxed setting, extensive menu selections, and inexpensive rates.

Conclusion

Plaza Bavaro provides a bustling and exciting shopping experience in the center of Bavaro, with a wide range of stores, food options, and entertainment venues to discover and enjoy. Visitors to Plaza Bavaro may enjoy Punta Cana's particular charm and character by shopping for souvenirs, eating local food, or simply soaking up the environment.

Higuey Market.

Higuey Market, commonly known as Mercado de Higuey, is a thriving marketplace in the village of Higuey, just a short drive from Punta Cana. This colorful market allows tourists to experience true Dominican culture while shopping for local items, fresh fruit, and traditional crafts.

Local Produce and Goods

Higuey Market is a thriving hive of activity where tourists may experience the sights, sounds, and scents of Dominican daily life. The market is packed with colorful vendors offering fresh fruits, vegetables, herbs, spices, and other locally grown food. Visitors may try exotic fruits including mangoes, papayas, pineapples, and passion fruit, as well as buy components for traditional Dominican meals.

In addition to fresh fruit, Higuey Market sells a range of other goods and commodities, such as home items, apparel, accessories, and gadgets. Visitors may peruse the stalls and dealers, negotiating and bargaining for deals and discounts on a variety of things.

Traditional Crafts and Artwork

One of the features of Higuey Market is its collection of traditional crafts and artisanal items manufactured by local artists and craftsmen. Pottery, ceramics, woven baskets, wooden sculptures, and handcrafted jewelry are among the unique and handmade objects on display for visitors.

Artisans at Higuey Market frequently showcase their craft talents, allowing tourists to witness as they produce beautiful and detailed products with traditional techniques and processes. Visitors may purchase one-of-a-kind souvenirs and keepsakes to remember their journey to the Dominican Republic.

Cultural Experience

Visiting Higuey Market provides tourists with a one-of-a-kind cultural experience, allowing them to mingle with local sellers, craftsmen, and inhabitants in a vibrant and genuine environment. Visitors may practice their Spanish, learn about Dominican customs and traditions, and enjoy the market's colorful environment.

Exploring Higuey Market provides an opportunity to learn about the everyday lives and business of Dominican villages and settlements, away from the tourist resorts and beaches of Punta Cana. Visitors may observe the hustle and bustle of market life, as merchants sell their items and consumers bargain for the best deals, resulting in a lively and dynamic atmosphere.

Tips for Visiting the Higuey Market

- Arrive early in the morning to see the market at its busiest and most vibrant.

- Wear comfortable shoes and clothing because the market might be congested and hot.

- Bring cash in small amounts, as some businesses may not take credit cards.

- Be prepared to haggle and bargain pricing, as this is standard practice in Dominican marketplaces.

- Respect the merchants and their products, and obtain permission before snapping images.

Overall, visiting Higuey Market gives tourists with a fascinating view into Dominican culture, as well as the opportunity to purchase for local items, sample fresh vegetables, and engage with local craftsmen and people in an authentic and immersive environment.

Souvenir Shops and Artisan Market

In addition to the major shopping malls and traditional markets, Punta Cana has a number of souvenir stores and artisan markets where travelers may buy one-of-a-kind souvenirs, keepsakes, and memorabilia to remember their vacation to the Dominican Republic.

Local Souvenir Shops

Souvenir stores can be found all across Punta Cana, making it easy for guests to buy presents and mementos. These stores often sell t-shirts, caps, keychains, magnets, postcards, and other goods bearing distinctive Punta Cana and Dominican Republic motifs.

Visitors may peruse the stores and booths, looking for the ideal gift to take home as a remembrance of their stay in paradise. Whether you're buying for friends, family, or yourself, Punta Cana's souvenir stores provide something for everyone.

Artisan marketplaces

Artisan fairs are ideal for individuals looking for one-of-a-kind, handmade items. These markets comprise stalls and booths showing the work of local artisans and craftsmen, offering a diverse selection of handcrafted items including pottery, ceramics, textiles, jewellery, artwork, and home décor.

Artisan markets allow tourists to support local craftsmen while purchasing original, one-of-a-kind creations that embody the beauty and character of the Dominican Republic. Visitors may see craftsmen showcase their craft skills and learn about ancient techniques and procedures that have been passed down through centuries.

Tips for Shopping at Souvenir Shops and Artisan Markets

- Take your time exploring the stores and booths; there might be hidden gems waiting to be uncovered.

- Don't be hesitant to haggle and negotiate prices, especially in artisan markets where bargaining is customary.

- Ask questions and interact with the craftsmen and dealers to understand more about their work and the stories behind it.

- Before purchase, thoroughly inspect the products to confirm their quality and originality.

- Consider buying presents and souvenirs that benefit local communities and artists, such as handcrafted crafts and artisanal goods.

Overall, shopping in Punta Cana's souvenir stores and artisan markets is a joyful and rewarding experience, allowing travelers to purchase unique and meaningful presents while also supporting local craftsmen and companies. Visitors to Punta Cana will appreciate the retail environment, whether they are looking for souvenirs, handmade treasures, or simply soaking up the colorful vibe.

Chapter 9

NIGHTLIFE & ENTERTAINMENT IN PUNTA CANA.

Punta Cana is recognized not just for its beautiful beaches and opulent resorts, but also for its active nightlife and entertainment offerings. From beach parties and bars to nightclubs and live music venues, this tropical paradise has something for everyone to enjoy once the sun goes down.

In this chapter, we'll look at the best nightlife and entertainment spots in Punta Cana.

Beach Party and Bar

Punta Cana's beaches come alive after dark, with a thriving party scene that draws travelers from all over the world. Beach bars and clubs border the coastline, providing a vibrant environment, tropical drinks, and throbbing music to keep the party going late into the night.

Beach Bars

Beach bars are a popular nightlife choice in Punta Cana, providing a casual and laid-back ambiance in which guests may drink cocktails, dig their toes in the sand, and admire stunning views of the Caribbean Sea. Many beach bars provide live music, DJ sets, and special events like bonfires, fire dance, and themed parties to enhance the celebratory atmosphere.

Visitors may dance beneath the stars, connect with other visitors, and soak up the tropical sensations while sipping cool cocktails and feeling the warm Caribbean wind. Whether you're reclining on a beach chair or dancing barefoot on the sand, beach bars provide a must-see Punta Cana evening experience.

Beach parties.

In addition to beach bars, Punta Cana is known for its legendary beach parties, which attract large groups of revelers seeking to dance the night away beneath the stars. From full moon parties to seaside raves, there's always a party going on along Punta Cana's shoreline.

Beach parties frequently include live DJs, dancers, entertainers, and extravagant light shows, which create an electric atmosphere brimming with energy and excitement. Visitors may participate in the celebrations, make new friends, and create memories that will last a lifetime while dancing to the latest sounds and soaking in the party atmosphere on the beach.

Tips for Beach Parties and Bars

- Dress comfortably and informally, as beachwear is the standard.

- Bring sunscreen because many beach parties and bars are outside and exposed to the sun.

- Arrive early to get the best place on the beach or near the dance floor.

- Stay hydrated by alternating between alcoholic beverages and water.

- Please respect the beach environment and dispose of waste appropriately.

Overall, beach parties and bars provide guests with an enjoyable and memorable nightlife experience in Punta Cana, allowing them to dance, drink, and celebrate beneath the stars with old and new friends.

Clubs and Discotheques

For those eager to dance the night away to the latest sounds and hottest tunes, Punta Cana has many world-class nightclubs and discotheques catering to a wide spectrum of musical interests and preferences.

Popular nightclubs

Punta Cana's nightclubs are renowned for their high-energy atmosphere, cutting-edge sound systems, and world-class DJs that keep the dance floor full until the early hours of the morning. Whether you prefer electronic dance music, reggaeton, hip-hop, or Latin sounds, there's a nightclub in Punta Cana for you.

Popular Punta Cana nightclubs frequently host themed parties, star guest DJs, and special events that draw partygoers from all over the world. Visitors may anticipate VIP bottle service, private lounges, and lavish decor to provide an elite and exclusive partying experience.

Local discotheques

In addition to international nightclubs, Punta Cana has various local discotheques and dance clubs where guests may enjoy the thriving Dominican nightlife scene. These establishments provide a more personal and genuine ambiance, with local DJs presenting a mix of salsa, merengue, bachata, and reggaeton music that draws both locals and visitors to the dance floor.

Local discotheques frequently offer live bands, dance performances, and cultural presentations celebrating the Dominican Republic's rich musical heritage and traditions. Visitors may immerse themselves in the rhythms and sounds of Dominican music, learn new dance skills, and enjoy the warm and welcoming atmosphere of the local nightlife scene.

Tips for nightclubs and discos

- Check the dress code before going out, since certain nightclubs have rigorous dress codes.

- Arrive early to prevent excessive wait times and cover costs.

- Bring a valid ID, as many nightclubs have age limits and may need identification to enter.

- Pace yourself and drink wisely to guarantee a safe and pleasurable evening out.

- Respect other clubgoers and adhere to the club's rules and regulations.

Overall, nightclubs and discotheques in Punta Cana provide guests with an interesting and memorable nightlife experience, allowing them to dance, mingle, and party the night away in style.

Live Music Venues.

Punta Cana has a number of live music venues where tourists may see performances by local bands, musicians, and artists representing a wide range of musical genres and styles.

Beachfront Bars and Restaurants.

Many coastal cafes and restaurants in Punta Cana provide live music performances, giving tourists a relaxing and private atmosphere to enjoy the sounds of acoustic guitar, Caribbean steel drums, or traditional merengue and bachata music. Visitors may enjoy beverages, dine on fresh seafood, and relax to the calming strains of live music set against the backdrop of the ocean.

Music Festivals and Events

Throughout the year, Punta Cana stages a number of music festivals and events that highlight local and international artists from a variety of musical genres. From jazz and blues festivals to electronic dance music events and reggae performances, there is always something going on in Punta Cana for music fans to enjoy.

Music festivals frequently include many stages, food and beverage vendors, art exhibits, and other entertainment options that create a lively and dynamic environment for guests. Visitors may dance, sing, and celebrate their love of music among other fans from all around the world.

Local Bars and Clubs

In addition to beachside venues and music festivals, Punta Cana has a number of local pubs, clubs, and lounges that provide live music performances by excellent local bands and musicians. These venues allow tourists to discover new music, support local artists, and become immersed in the Dominican Republic's thriving music culture.

Whether you enjoy jazz, rock, reggae, or traditional Dominican music, Punta Cana has a live music venue to suit your interests. Visitors may enjoy a night of live music, dancing, and entertainment, soaking in the sounds and rhythms of the Caribbean and making memories that last a lifetime.

Tips for Live Music Venues.

- Check local listings and event calendars for upcoming live music shows and activities.

- Arrive early to ensure a decent location near the stage.

- Help local bands by buying goods or CDs.

- During performances, be considerate to both the artists and your fellow audience members.

- Enjoy the music and have fun!

Overall, live music venues in Punta Cana provide guests with a lively and immersive nightlife experience, allowing them to explore new sounds, dance to the beat, and celebrate their love of music in paradise.

Dinner Shows And Cultural Performances.

Dinner shows and cultural acts provide a riveting combination of entertainment, cuisine, and culture that celebrates the Dominican Republic's rich past and customs, making for a one-of-a-kind and memorable nighttime experience in Punta Cana. Dinner shows and cultural events provide tourists an immersive and enlightening experience of Dominican culture, including traditional dances and music, dramatic acts, and interactive activities.

Traditional Dominican Dinner Shows.

One of the most popular types of entertainment in Punta Cana is the traditional Dominican dinner show, which includes a great meal as well as live music, dancing performances, and cultural presentations. These dinner presentations, which take place in resorts, restaurants, or event locations, provide tourists a taste of real Dominican food and hospitality.

During a traditional Dominican dinner performance, guests may expect to try a range of local delicacies like as plantains, yuca, rice and beans, roasted meats, and seafood, all served with tropical drinks and refreshing beverages. Throughout the dinner, live musicians entertain guests with traditional music, while dancers perform lively and colorful routines featuring the rhythms and motions of merengue, bachata, and salsa.

Guests may also be able to participate in participatory activities such as dancing classes, drum circles, or storytelling sessions, which allow them to connect with Dominican culture in a fun and hands-on way. Whether it's a romantic meal for two or a raucous group celebration, traditional Dominican dinner performances provide a wonderful evening of entertainment and cultural immersion.

Theatrical performances and shows.

In addition to typical dinner shows, Punta Cana offers a range of theatrical performances and shows that highlight the brilliance and inventiveness of local artists and entertainers. These presentations may include theater plays, musicals, comedy acts, magic shows, and others, giving tourists a wide selection of entertainment alternatives to choose from.

Theaters in Punta Cana frequently offer cutting-edge equipment, skilled production teams, and complex sets and costumes to create an immersive and unique theatrical experience. Pre-show festivities include meet-and-greets, picture opportunities, and backstage tours, in addition to performances by local and international performers.

Cultural Festivals and Events

Throughout the year, Punta Cana offers a number of cultural festivals and events to showcase the Dominican Republic's unique heritage and traditions. These festivals may feature music and dance performances, art exhibitions, culinary demonstrations, artisan fairs, and other activities, providing visitors with a one-of-a-kind opportunity to experience Dominican culture in all of its richness and diversity.

From the colorful Carnival celebrations to the traditional music and dance festivals performed throughout the year, cultural activities in Punta Cana allow tourists to immerse themselves in Dominican culture's sights, sounds, and smells. Visitors may obtain a better understanding of the Dominican Republic's cultural history and inventiveness by tasting local foods, learning traditional dance techniques, and appreciating handcrafted artwork.

Tips for Dinner Shows and Cultural Performances.

- Make reservations early, especially for popular supper events and theatrical performances.

- Arrive early to locate parking and get a decent seat.

- Dress appropriately for the event, considering the location and dress code.

- Bring cash for tips, beverages, and souvenirs.

- Approach the performers with an open mind and appreciation for their talent.

Overall, Punta Cana's supper shows and cultural acts provide guests with a one-of-a-kind and unforgettable experience of the Dominican Republic's colorful culture and customs.

Chapter 10

DAYTRIPS FROM PUNTA CANA

Punta Cana, famed for its stunning beaches and active nightlife, is also a good starting point for visiting the surrounding areas and learning about the Dominican Republic's rich cultural and natural legacy.

In this chapter, we'll look at three must-see day trip sites from Punta Cana: Santo Domingo, Altos de Chavón, and the Samana Peninsula.

Santo Domingo.

Santo Domingo, the Dominican Republic's capital city, is a thriving metropolis with a rich history, intriguing architecture, and a dynamic culture. Santo Domingo, located about 200 kilometers west of Punta Cana, is readily accessible by vehicle, bus, or organized excursions, making it a great day trip destination for travelers wishing to immerse themselves in the country's rich cultural legacy.

Colonial Zone

One of Santo Domingo's features is its historic Colonial Zone, a UNESCO World Heritage Site that protects the city's colonial architecture and landmarks. Visitors may stroll down cobblestone streets lined with colorful buildings, see centuries-old churches and cathedrals, and see historic plazas and monuments that reflect the narrative of the city's colonial past.

The Alcázar de Colón, the historic home of Christopher Columbus' son Diego, is now a museum that displays colonial relics and artwork. Another must-see attraction is the Catedral Primada de América, the Americas' oldest cathedral, known for its Gothic and Baroque architectural styles.

Cultural Attractions

In addition to its historic landmarks, Santo Domingo has a plethora of cultural attractions, including museums, galleries, and theaters. The Museo de las Casas Reales, Museo de Arte Moderno, and Centro Cultural de España offer opportunities to learn about the country's history and art.

Visitors may get a taste of local life by exploring Santo Domingo's lively streets and marketplaces, where they can eat traditional Dominican food, shop for handicrafts and souvenirs, and mingle with the residents. The Malecón, a picturesque waterfront promenade, provides breathtaking views of the Caribbean Sea and is a favorite site for leisurely strolls and people-watching.

Shopping and Dining

Santo Domingo also has a thriving culinary culture with a diverse range of dining options, from street food sellers and local eateries to fancy restaurants and foreign cuisine. Visitors may enjoy classic Dominican delicacies like mofongo, sancocho, and tostones, as well as fresh fish and tropical fruits.

Santo Domingo has a wide range of shopping malls, shops, and marketplaces where travelers may purchase anything from designer clothing and jewelry to homemade crafts and souvenirs. The Mercado Modelo, one of the city's most well-known marketplaces, is an excellent spot to buy local artwork, cigars, and handicrafts.

Conclusion

A day journey to Santo Domingo from Punta Cana provides an intriguing peek into the history, culture, and legacy of the Dominican Republic's capital.

Altos de Chavón

Altos de Chavón is a lovely Mediterranean-style community located high above the Chavón River in the eastern Dominican Republic. It serves as the region's cultural and artistic core. Altos de Chavón, created in the late 1970s by Italian architect Roberto Copa and Dominican designer Oscar de la Renta, is a one-of-a-kind and lovely location that combines history, art, and breathtaking vistas.

Art and Culture

Altos de Chavón features a number of cultural attractions, including art galleries, studios, and workshops where tourists may view and purchase works by local and international artists. The town also holds cultural events and performances, such as concerts, art exhibitions, and theatrical shows, to highlight the skills of the Dominican Republic's creative population.

One of the features of Altos de Chavón is the Altos de Chavón School of Design, which is linked with the Parsons School of Design in New York City. The school provides studies in visual arts, design, and architecture, and it has produced many great artists and designers who have contributed significantly to the Dominican and international arts scenes.

Historic sites.

In addition to cultural attractions, Altos de Chavón has various historic sites and landmarks that offer insight into the village's past. The Altos de Chavón Archaeological Museum displays relics and exhibits about the indigenous Taíno people that lived in the region.

Another must-see attraction in Altos de Chavón is the St. Stanislaus Church, a copy of a 15th-century Mediterranean church that is both a popular wedding location and an architectural masterpiece. Visitors may take in the church's beautiful stone carvings, stained glass windows, and panoramic views of the surrounding landscape.

Scenic views and outdoor activities

Altos de Chavón is particularly well-known for its spectacular views of the Chavón River and surrounding landscapes, making it a favorite destination for photographers, tourists, and outdoor enthusiasts. Visitors may meander along the cobblestone streets, discover hidden lanes and courtyards, or unwind at one of the village's lovely cafes or eateries.

Outdoor enthusiasts may enjoy hiking, horseback riding, and river trips at Altos de Chavón, giving them a taste of the Dominican countryside's natural beauty and calm. Whether viewing the sunset across the river or touring the village's historic landmarks, Altos de Chavón provides a tranquil and scenic escape from the rush and bustle of Punta Cana.

Conclusion

A day excursion to Altos de Chavón from Punta Cana provides guests with a one-of-a-kind and captivating experience that mixes art, culture, and history in a picturesque Mediterranean-style hamlet environment. Visitors to Altos de Chavón will be attracted by its charm and beauty, whether they are perusing art galleries, seeing historic monuments, or simply taking in the scenery.

Samana Peninsula

The Samaná Peninsula, located on the Dominican Republic's northeast coast, is a pure and scenic location recognized for its natural beauty, lush landscapes, and lovely beaches. A day journey to the Samaná Peninsula from Punta Cana allows tourists to see some of the Dominican Republic's most beautiful natural features, such as waterfalls, national parks, and isolated coves.

Los Haitises National Park

Los Haitises National Park, a protected region with mangrove forests, limestone karst formations, and a vast network of caves and tunnels, is one of the Samaná Peninsula's attractions. Visitors may explore the park's different ecosystems via boat, kayak, or hiking paths, discovering secret caverns, gorgeous beaches, and plentiful animals along the way.

The park is home to a variety of bird species, including herons, egrets, pelicans, and frigatebirds, making it a favorite spot for birdwatchers. Visitors may learn about the park's history and cultural significance, since it was formerly home to the indigenous Taíno people and subsequently became a haven for pirates and buccaneers.

El Limón Waterfall

The El Limón Waterfall, a stunning cascade that plunges more than 50 meters into a blue pool below, is one of the Samaná Peninsula's most renowned natural attractions. The waterfall is located deep in the thick forest and may be reached via a picturesque stroll or horseback ride across the green landscape.

Visitors may take a guided excursion to El Limón cascade, where they will walk along winding pathways, cross wooden bridges, and wade through crystal-clear streams before reaching the beautiful cascade. Along the route, they'll come across exotic flora and animals, such as tropical flowers, towering palms, and colorful butterflies, adding to the sense of adventure and discovery.

Once at the waterfall, tourists may take a relaxing plunge in the cold, clear waters of the pool below, swim beneath the flowing falls, or simply relax and enjoy the natural beauty of the surrounds. Climbing to the top of the waterfall provides an exciting vantage point and sweeping views of the jungle canopy below.

Playa Rincón

For beach enthusiasts, a day excursion to Playa Rincón from Punta Cana is a must. Playa Rincón is widely recognized as one of the Dominican Republic's most beautiful beaches, with pure white sands, blue seas, and swaying palm trees that provide for a postcard-perfect backdrop for sunbathing, swimming, and snorkeling.

Visitors may spend the day lazing on the beach, enjoying the sun, and swimming in the Caribbean Sea's quiet, clear waters. Those looking for adventure may visit the adjacent coral reefs, which are home to a wide variety of aquatic life, including colorful fish, sea turtles, and stingrays.

Playa Rincón is particularly well-known for its delectable seafood restaurants and beach bars, where guests can enjoy freshly caught seafood, tropical cocktails, and refreshing drinks while taking in panoramic views of the beach and ocean. Whether lounging on the sand, snorkeling in the water, or enjoying a seafood feast, Playa Rincón provides tourists with a must-see Caribbean beach experience.

Whale Watching

From January to March, the seas off the Samaná Peninsula serve as a breeding area for humpback whales, who migrate from the North Atlantic to mate and give birth in warm Caribbean waters. A day excursion to Samaná during whale-watching season allows guests to see these spectacular creatures up close in their natural environment.

Visitors may go on a whale-watching expedition from Samaná, where skilled guides and boat captains take tours to the best whale-watching spots in the harbor. Visitors may be lucky enough to view humpback whales breaching, tail-slapping, and nursing their babies, delivering a once-in-a-lifetime wildlife experience that is both exhilarating and awe-inspiring.

Conclusion

A day journey from Punta Cana to the Samaná Peninsula allows tourists to discover some of the Dominican Republic's most beautiful natural features, including spectacular waterfalls and clean beaches, as well as vivid coral reefs and breathtaking wildlife encounters.

La Romea

La Romana, located on the Dominican Republic's southern coast, is a thriving city noted for its rich history, vibrant culture, and breathtaking scenery. A day excursion to La Romana from Punta Cana allows tourists to see ancient places, participate in outdoor activities, and discover the beauty of this vibrant city.

Altos de Chavón

Altos de Chavón, a lovely town positioned high above the Chavón River, is a La Romana must-see. Altos de Chavón, designed in the 1970s to imitate a 16th-century Mediterranean town, is a cultural and artistic hotspot with cobblestone lanes, stone structures, and attractive plazas.

Visitors to Altos de Chavón may tour art galleries, studios, and workshops that display the work of local and international artists. The hamlet also houses the Altos de Chavón School of Design, which is linked with the Parsons School of Design in New York City and offers visitors the opportunity to learn about the creative process and examine student artwork.

Casa de Campo

Casa de Campo is one of the most luxury resorts and residential communities in the Caribbean, located just outside of La Romana. Casa de Campo spans 7,000 acres and provides a variety of amenities and activities for tourists, including golf courses, tennis courts, equestrian centers, and marinas.

Visitors to Casa de Campo may enjoy a guided tour of the resort's features, which include the breathtaking Altos de Chavón amphitheater, the Teeth of the Dog golf course, and the Marina at Casa de Campo. Those seeking leisure can lay by the pool, receive spa treatments, or dine at one of the resort's restaurants.

Cave of the Maravillas

A day excursion from La Romana to the Cueva de las Maravillas (Cave of Wonders) is a must for history buffs. This vast cave system, located just outside the city, has about 500 petroglyphs and cave paintings from the pre-Columbian era, as well as stalactites and stalagmites produced millions of years ago.

Visitors to Cueva de las Maravillas may enjoy a guided tour of the caverns, which include chambers and corridors adorned with ancient artwork and geological formations. The cave system provides insight into the island's history and legacy, including the indigenous Taíno people that used to live there.

Conclusion

A day excursion from Punta Cana to La Romana allows tourists to see ancient monuments, engage in outdoor activities, and immerse themselves in the city's colorful culture.

El Limón Waterfall.

El Limón Waterfall, located deep in the lush woods of the Samaná Peninsula, is a beautiful natural wonder that provides a refreshing getaway from the heat and hustle of Punta Cana. A day excursion to El Limón Waterfall near Punta Cana allows guests to take a magnificent stroll or horseback ride through the tropical landscape, finishing in a refreshing dip beneath the flowing waterfalls.

Hike to El Limón Waterfall

The trek to El Limón Waterfall begins with a picturesque stroll through the lush forest, traversing winding routes and crossing wooden bridges along the way. Visitors may take in panoramic views of the surrounding landscapes, listen to unusual bird and mammal calls, and learn about the region's flora and fauna from professional guides.

As the trek advances, the waterfall's roar becomes louder, signifying the approach to the major feature. Visitors will travel over tough terrain and drop into a green canyon before emerging at the base of the waterfall, where they will be rewarded with breathtaking views of the tumbling falls and the crystal-clear lake below.

Horseback Riding Adventure

For those looking for a more leisurely trip to El Limón Waterfall, horseback riding is a popular and picturesque choice. Visitors may saddle up and ride across the countryside, passing through tiny villages and crossing rivers to experience the sights and sounds of rural Dominican life.

Along the route, helpful guides will provide anecdotes and insights into the region's history and culture, pointing out landmarks and offering assistance as required. When riders approach the waterfall, they may dismount and have a relaxing plunge in the cool, clear waters of the pool below, surrounded by the lush splendor of the rainforest.

Swimming and Relaxation

Once at the waterfall, guests can take a break from their trek or horseback ride to rest and appreciate the natural beauty of the surrounds. The pool behind the waterfall provides a welcome relief from the heat, enticing tourists to swim, splash, and cool down in the crystal clear waters.

Visitors may also rest on the rocks that surround the pool, sunbathe on the beach, or eat a picnic lunch amidst the peaceful sounds of nature. El Limón Waterfall, with its towering waterfall as a background, is the ideal location for a fantastic day of adventure and leisure in the heart of the Dominican Republic.

Conclusion

A day excursion to El Limón Waterfall from Punta Cana allows guests to enjoy the natural beauty and quiet of the Dominican Republic's rich jungle settings.

Chapter 11

FAMILY-FRIENDLY ACTIVITIES IN PUNTA CANA

Punta Cana is not just an adult paradise, but it also has a variety of family-friendly activities that appeal to people of all ages. From thrilling water parks and engaging dolphin encounters to daring ziplining excursions, there are plenty of exciting activities for families to do together.

In this chapter, we'll look at three popular family-friendly activities in Punta Cana: water parks and amusement parks, dolphin discovery, and zipline adventures.

Waterparks and Amusement Centers

Punta Cana has various amazing water parks and amusement parks that provide unlimited entertainment for family wishing to escape the heat and have some fun in the sun. These parks have a range of activities, such as water slides, wave pools, lazy rivers, and more, assuring a day of excitement and adventure for guests of all ages.

Sirenis Aquagames Punta Cana

Sirenis Aquagames Punta Cana is one of the Caribbean's largest water parks, with a variety of attractions and activities for the entire family to enjoy. The park has exhilarating water slides including the Kamikaze, Black Hole, and Free Fall, as well as a soothing lazy river, wave pool, and children's play area.

Visitors may spend the day speeding down water slides, swimming in pools, and basking in the tropical sunlight. The park also has restaurants, snack bars, and gift stores, allowing families to spend the full day enjoying all Sirenis Aquagames has to offer.

Bavaro Adventure Park

Bávaro Adventure Park is another famous family-friendly destination in Punta Cana, providing a variety of activities and experiences for people of all ages. Zip lines, bungee jumping, rope courses, and climbing walls are among the attractions of the park, which also offers horseback riding, paintball, and off-road buggy trips.

Families may spend the day exploring the park's rich surroundings, participating in adrenaline-pumping challenges, and experiencing exhilarating outdoor activities together. With possibilities for both small children and ambitious teenagers, Bávaro Adventure Park has something for everyone in the family to enjoy.

Tips for visiting water parks and amusement centers

- Arrive early to beat the throng and get a decent seat.

- Wear sunblock and remain hydrated all day.

- Follow the safety regulations and recommendations for each attraction.

- Pack towels, swimsuits, and a change of clothes for after your water activities.

- Consider getting a multi-day pass to have unrestricted access to the park's attractions.

Overall, water parks and amusement parks in Punta Cana offer families a fun and thrilling opportunity to cool down while making lifelong memories together in paradise.

Dolphin Discovery.

Dolphin Discovery provides families with a unique and interactive experience by allowing them to swim and interact with dolphins in their natural habitat. Dolphin Discovery has multiple sites in Punta Cana and offers a secure and instructive atmosphere in which tourists may learn about these clever marine creatures and make great experiences with their families.

Dolphin Encounter

Dolphin Encounter programs enable guests to go into shallow water and interact with dolphins in a comfortable and regulated environment. Participants may pet, kiss, and play with the dolphins while also learning about their natural environment and behaviors from qualified trainers.

Dolphin Swim

Dolphin Swim programs provide a more immersive experience, with people swimming with dolphins in deeper water. Visitors may engage in activities like as dorsal fin rides, belly rides, and underwater interactions with these gorgeous creatures while also learning about their biology, conservation, and care.

Dolphin Trainer for the Day

Dolphin Discovery provides the Dolphin Trainer for a Day program, which allows people to follow a trainer and assist with the dolphins' care and training. This hands-on experience gives participants an inside look at dolphin trainers' daily routines and duties, as well as an opportunity to form a stronger bond with these amazing animals.

Tips for visiting Dolphin Discovery

- Reserve your adventure in advance, as places fill up rapidly, particularly during busy tourist seasons.

- Wear sunscreen, a hat, and sunglasses to protect your skin from the sun.

- Follow the trainers' and staff's directions to ensure a safe and pleasurable experience.

- Bring a waterproof camera or GoPro to record images and videos of your encounters with the dolphins.

- Take advantage of Dolphin Discovery's picture packages to cherish your memories.

Overall, Dolphin Discovery provides families with an unforgettable opportunity to engage with dolphins while learning about marine conservation in a fun and engaging way.

Zip Lining Adventures

Ziplining trips in Punta Cana are an exciting opportunity for families looking for adventure and adrenaline-pumping thrills to enjoy the region's breathtaking landscapes and natural beauty from a new viewpoint. Families may soar through the treetops, zip across rivers and valleys, and take in spectacular vistas of the Dominican countryside thanks to various zipline businesses that provide tours and excursions.

Runners Adventure Zip Line

Runners Adventures Zip Line provides a thrilling zipline ride through Punta Cana's gorgeous forest canopy. The trip includes many ziplines of varied lengths and heights, as well as suspension bridges and platforms with panoramic views of the surrounding area.

Participants may zip through the treetops, soar over rivers and ravines, and experience a sense of excitement while navigating the course. The trip also offers opportunity to learn about the local flora and wildlife from professional guides, making it both entertaining and instructive for families.

Canopy Adventure Zip Line

Canopy Adventure Zip Line provides another thrilling zipline adventure in Punta Cana, with trips taking passengers through the Anamuya Mountains and Rainforest. The trip includes many ziplines, including the exhilarating Superman zipline, which allows riders to glide through the air in a horizontal position, Tarzan swings, and a rope bridge.

Participants may experience breathtaking views of the surrounding regions, which include lush woods, tumbling waterfalls, and panoramic panoramas. The tour also provides opportunities to see wildlife such as tropical birds, iguanas, and butterflies, which adds to the excitement and adventure of the journey.

Tips For Ziplining Adventures

- Dress comfortably for outdoor activities and wear closed-toed shoes

- Follow the safety rules and recommendations issued by the trip organizers.

- Secure any loose things, such as cameras, phones, and caps, to keep them from dropping during the zipline.

- Pack sunscreen, bug repellent, and a reusable water bottle to remain hydrated during the trip.

- If you want a more personalized experience, schedule a private or semi-private tour.

Overall, ziplining activities in Punta Cana provide families with an exciting and amazing opportunity to see the region's natural beauties and sceneries from a new viewpoint.

Conclusion

Punta Cana has a variety of family-friendly activities and attractions for guests of all ages, including thrilling water parks, engaging dolphin encounters, and daring ziplining tours.

Pirate Ship Excursions

Punta Cana provides families with the opportunity to go on exciting pirate ship excursions, where they may set sail on replica pirate ships and experience a swashbuckling adventure on the open sea. These trips mix exhilarating activities, captivating entertainment, and breathtaking scenery to provide families with an unforgettable experience.

Pirate Show

Pirate ship trips usually start with a colorful pirate entertainment aboard the ship, which includes costumed actors, music, and theatrical acts that set the tone for the adventure ahead. Families may witness pirates fight in mock battles, perform acrobatics, and amuse guests with their pranks, resulting in an immersive and engaging experience for all ages.

Treasure hunts

Once underway, pirate ship tours frequently feature participatory treasure hunts and family-friendly activities. Guests may be given maps, clues, and puzzles to answer while searching for hidden treasure on the ship, participating in friendly competition and collaboration along the way.

Swimming and snorkelling

Many pirate ship trips feature opportunities to swim and snorkel in the Caribbean Sea's crystal-clear waters. The ship may moor in a remote cove or reef, allowing families to wear snorkel gear and explore the underwater world, discovering brilliant coral reefs, tropical fish, and other marine life.

Dining and refreshments.

During the expedition, family may have great aboard meals or snacks, which are frequently provided buffet-style or as part of a themed pirate feast. Refreshments such as tropical drinks, sodas, and water are often provided, keeping guests hydrated and invigorated during the journey.

Entertainment and Activities

In addition to the pirate entertainment and treasure hunts, pirate ship excursions may include live music, dancing, and games to keep passengers engaged during the cruise. Families may participate in the fun by taking part in limbo contests, pirate-themed quizzes, and other interactive games that add to the excitement and enjoyment of the event.

Tips for Pirate Ship Excursions.

- Reserve your journey in advance, since space may be limited, particularly during busy tourist seasons.

- Bring sunscreen, hats, and sunglasses to protect yourself from the sun's rays when on deck.

- Dress comfortably and appropriately for walking and swimming.

- Bring a camera or a waterproof case to record images and videos of your journey.

- Be prepared to experience some motion nausea, particularly if you are prone to seasickness.

Overall, pirate ship excursions in Punta Cana provide families with an exciting and engaging experience that mixes adventure, entertainment, and relaxation on the high seas.

Ecotours and Animal Encounters

Eco-tours and animal encounters are ideal for families looking to see Punta Cana's natural beauty and animals. Every environment enthusiast may enjoy guided nature walks and birding trips, as well as visits to wildlife sanctuaries and conservation institutions.

Monkeyland

Monkeyland is a famous eco-tourism site in Punta Cana, where families may take guided excursions through beautiful jungle settings and interact with energetic and sociable squirrel monkeys. Visitors may learn about monkey behavior, ecology, and conservation initiatives while feeding and photographing these cute critters in their natural setting.

Punta Cana Ecological Reserve

The Punta Cana Ecological Reserve allows families to explore beautiful tropical forests, mangrove swamps, and freshwater lagoons abounding with animals. Guided tours of the reserve allow visitors to observe local flora and animals, such as colorful birds, reptiles, and amphibians, while also learning about the significance of conservation and environmental stewardship.

Manatí Park

Manatí Park is a family-friendly destination that offers entertainment, education, and conservation in a lush tropical environment. Visitors may see interactive animal shows with dolphins, sea lions, and exotic birds, as well as visit botanical gardens, indigenous communities, and petting zoos that highlight the region's cultural and ecological history.

Horseback Riding Tours

Horseback riding trips give families a more active vacation, allowing them to discover Punta Cana's stunning landscapes and beaches on horseback. Guided excursions transport guests through lush woods, sandy pathways, and beautiful beaches, allowing them to observe animals, savor panoramic vistas, and relax in nature.

Tips for Ecotours and Animal Encounters

- Choose eco-tours and animal interactions that put animal care and conservation first.

- Follow the tour guides' and staff's directions to guarantee everyone's safety and enjoyment.

- Respect wildlife and natural environments by viewing animals from a distance and without feeding or touching them.

- Bring binoculars, cameras, and bug repellent to improve your wildlife viewing experience.

- Support local conservation efforts and sustainable tourism practices by selecting eco-friendly tour operators and sites.

Overall, eco-tours and animal encounters in Punta Cana allow families to reconnect with nature, learn about conservation, and make great experiences together in paradise.

Chapter 12

WELLNESS AND RELAXATION AT PUNTA CANA

Punta Cana is not only an adventure and thrill hotspot, but also a health and relaxation sanctuary. Punta Cana's gorgeous beaches, lush scenery, and calm ambiance make it the ideal place to rejuvenate the mind, body, and spirit.

In this chapter, we'll look at four popular methods to relax and indulge in wellness activities in Punta Cana: spa retreats and wellness centers, yoga and meditation classes, beachfront massages and relaxation, and nature walks and ecotherapy.

Spa Retreats and Wellness Centres

Punta Cana is home to a number of magnificent spa resorts and wellness centers that provide a variety of treatments and therapies aimed at promoting relaxation, renewal, and overall well-being. Everyone may find something they prefer, from classic massages and facials to holistic treatments and health rituals.

Six Senses Spa at Eden Roc Cap Cana.

The Six Senses Spa, located within the magnificent Eden Roc Cap Cana resort, provides a serene refuge for visitors to escape the worries of daily life and embark on a journey of relaxation and regeneration. The spa offers a variety of holistic treatments and therapies inspired by ancient medicinal traditions from throughout the world, such as massages, facials, and body scrubs.

Guests may relax at the spa's quiet settings, which include beautiful gardens, tranquil pools, and individual treatment rooms that overlook the Caribbean Sea. Signature treatments, such as the Punta Cana Massage, blend Swedish massage methods with locally sourced products like coconut oil and fragrant herbs to provide a completely immersive and delicious experience.

Zentropía Palladium Spa and Wellness.

The Zentropía Palladium Spa & Wellness center of the Grand Palladium Bavaro Suites Resort & Spa provides a variety of spa treatments and wellness services to encourage relaxation, balance, and harmony. Guests may select from a variety of massages, body treatments, facials, and beauty services, as well as use the spa's thermal circuit, which includes a sauna, steam room, and hydrotherapy pool.

The spa also provides yoga and meditation sessions, fitness programs, and wellness workshops taught by professional educators and practitioners. Guests can take group courses or plan private sessions based on their own requirements and preferences, delivering a personalized and transformational health experience.

Tips for Spas and Wellness Centers

- Schedule treatments and services in advance to ensure your chosen appointment times.

- Arrive early to take use of spa amenities including saunas, steam rooms, and relaxation lounges.

- Tell the therapist about your preferences, as well as any health issues or sensitivities, to ensure a safe and enjoyable session.

- Keep yourself hydrated before and after treatments by drinking lots of water.

- Take time to unwind and enjoy the moments of peace and renewal provided by your spa experience.

Overall, spa retreats and wellness centers in Punta Cana provide the ideal chance to relax, revitalize, and nourish your body, mind, and soul amidst the beauty and peace of the Caribbean.

Yoga and Meditation Classes.

Punta Cana provides a range of yoga and meditation programs for individuals seeking inner peace and spiritual refreshment amidst the region's gorgeous natural landscapes and calm environs. Whether practicing on the beach, in a beautiful garden, or in a tranquil studio, guests may connect with their breath, find calm inside, and create a sense of awareness and present.

Yoga Loft

The Yoga Loft, located in Punta Cana's Corales Golf Course enclave, provides a tranquil and friendly environment for practitioners of all skill levels to discover the transforming power of yoga together. The studio provides a range of programs, including Vinyasa flow, Hatha, Yin, and Kundalini yoga, as well as meditation and breathwork.

Guests may practice yoga surrounded by beautiful gardens, swaying palm trees, and panoramic views of the Caribbean Sea, creating a tranquil and inspirational environment for their practice. Experienced teachers offer workshops that focus on alignment, mindfulness, and self-awareness, fostering a supportive and loving atmosphere for personal development and transformation.

Yoga at the Beach

Many Punta Cana resorts and hotels offer beachside yoga programs, enabling guests to connect with nature and the calming sounds of the ocean. Sunrise and sunset yoga sessions are especially popular, since they provide opportunity to begin or finish the day with a sense of grounding, tranquility, and thankfulness.

Practicing yoga on the beach offers a unique sensory experience, with the feel of the sand between your feet, the sound of the waves smashing on the coast, and the warmth of the sun on your skin all contributing to a stronger mind-body connection and deeper practice. Whether you're doing sun salutations, grounding postures, or simply sitting in silent meditation, yoga on the beach is a truly nourishing and transformational experience.

Tips for Yoga and Meditation Classes

- Bring a yoga mat, towel, and water bottle to ensure you stay comfortable and hydrated during your practice.

- Dress in lightweight, breathable attire appropriate for yoga and meditation.

- Arrive early to set up your spot and relax before class starts.

- Listen to your body and respect its limitations, altering postures as needed to accommodate your degree of flexibility and strength.

- Take the time to center yourself and build a sense of presence and awareness throughout your practice.

Overall, yoga and meditation sessions in Punta Cana allow you to achieve inner serenity, balance, and harmony while enjoying the beauty and calm of the Caribbean.

Beachside Massages and Relaxation

Punta Cana's gorgeous beaches and calm shoreline make the ideal setting for luxurious beachside massages and relaxation activities. Whether you choose a classic massage under a swaying palm tree or a revitalizing spa treatment in a seaside cabana, there are several alternatives available to help you relieve stress and tension while listening to the calming sounds of the ocean.

Beach massage cabanas

Many resorts and hotels in Punta Cana have beach massage services, allowing customers to relax directly on the sand. Imagine yourself laying on a comfy massage table beneath a covered cabana, enjoying the lovely coastal air and listening to the rhythmic sound of the waves while professional therapists perform their magic, massaging away knots and stress in your muscles.

Beach massages often include a number of methods, including Swedish, deep tissue, and hot stone massage, that are personalized to your specific tastes and needs. A beach massage in Punta Cana is ideal for relieving aching muscles, reducing tension, or simply enjoying a moment of pure relaxation.

Spa Treatments at the Sea

For those seeking a more opulent spa experience, numerous Punta Cana resorts provide spa treatments and rituals in intimate beachside locations. Imagine indulging yourself with a luxury body scrub, wrap, or facial while sitting in a cabana overlooking the Caribbean Sea's turquoise seas, surrounded by natural sights and sounds.

Spa treatments near the sea frequently use natural substances available locally, such as sea salt, coconut oil, and aloe vera, to nourish and moisturize the skin. Skilled therapists employ mild massage methods to promote relaxation and general well-being, leaving you feeling revived, invigorated, and regenerated from head to toe.

Tips for Beachfront Massages and Relaxation

- Plan your beach massage or spa treatment during low tide to prevent disruptions from waves or high water levels.

- Communicate your preferences and any areas of tension or sensitivity to your therapist in order to provide a personalized and pleasurable treatment.

- Stay hydrated by drinking lots of water before and after your massage or spa session, especially if you're out in the sun.

- Wear sunscreen and reapply it periodically to protect your skin from sunburn when relaxing on the beach.

- During your massage or spa treatment, take the time to enjoy the views, sounds, and feelings of the seaside setting.

Overall, beachside massages and relaxation experiences in Punta Cana provide a delightful opportunity to unwind, revitalize, and reconnect with the natural beauty and quiet of the Caribbean shoreline.

Nature Walks and Ecotherapy

Punta Cana's lush landscapes, tropical forests, and pristine nature reserves make an ideal location for immersive nature walks and eco-therapy activities that encourage relaxation, renewal, and a stronger connection with nature. There are several possibilities to experience the therapeutic advantages of nature in Punta Cana, whether it is by hiking picturesque paths, viewing animals, or simply taking in the beauty of the surroundings.

Punta Cana Ecological Reserve

The Punta Cana Ecological Reserve is a massive protected area including over 1,500 acres of natural tropical forest, marshes, and shoreline. Guided nature walks and eco-tours allow visitors to explore the reserve's different ecosystems, witness local flora and wildlife, and learn about conservation efforts to preserve the region's natural legacy.

Trained guides accompany visitors down picturesque paths, pointing out unusual plant and animal species, imparting information about the area's ecology and biodiversity, and providing chances for quiet thought and contemplation amidst the splendor of the forest. Whether birding, hiking, or simply enjoying nature's quiet stillness, a visit to the Punta Cana Ecological Reserve provides a restorative getaway from the rush and bustle of daily life.

Indigenous Eyes Ecological Park and Reserve.

The Indigenous Eyes Ecological Park and Reserve, located within the Punta Cana Resort & Club, is a hidden gem where tourists may explore a network of paths, lagoons, and natural springs surrounded by beautiful tropical foliage. The park is home to a rich range of flora and wildlife, including native trees, orchids, and freshwater fish, as well as many bird species including herons, egrets, and woodpeckers.

Visitors can take self-guided walks or guided tours of the park, following well-marked paths that weave through the forest and around the park's 12 freshwater lagoons, dubbed "eyes" because of their crystal-clear waters. Along the trip, guests may enjoy spectacular views of the surrounding landscapes, listen to nature's noises, and relax in this natural refuge.

Tips for Nature Walks and Ecotherapy

- Wear comfortable walking shoes and light attire appropriate for outdoor activities.

- Pack bug repellent, sunscreen, and a reusable water bottle to be comfortable and hydrated on your nature walk.

- Bring a camera or smartphone to photograph the landscapes, wildlife, and distinctive elements of the area.

- Use mindfulness and deep breathing methods to strengthen your bond with nature and promote relaxation and stress alleviation.

- During your eco-therapy session, take time to pause, contemplate, and appreciate the natural environment's beauty and peace.

Overall, nature walks and eco-therapy activities in Punta Cana are a relaxing and refreshing way to reconnect with nature, nourish your spirit, and restore balance and harmony to your mind, body, and soul.

Chapter 13

HISTORIC AND CULTURAL WALKING TOURS

Exploring Punta Cana's rich history and lively culture is an exciting adventure that can be enjoyed on a variety of historical and cultural walking excursions. From ancient indigenous villages to colonial-era architecture and current heritage sites, Punta Cana has a wide range of attractions that highlight its distinct past and cultural character.

In this chapter, we'll look at four fascinating walking excursions that give insight into Punta Cana's historical and cultural significance: the Altos de Chavón Village Tour, the Higuey City Tour, the Indigenous Eyes Ecological Park Guided Walk, and the Dominican Republic Heritage Tour.

Altos de Chavón Village Tour

Altos de Chavón, located high above the Chavón River in the Dominican Republic, is a beautifully created recreation of a

16th-century Mediterranean town. This lovely hamlet was designed by Italian architect Roberto Copa and Dominican architect Jose Antonio Caro to serve as a living museum of Dominican culture and history.

Highlights from the Altos de Chavón Village Tour:

Chavón River: The journey frequently begins with a lovely stroll along the banks of the Chavón River, which provides panoramic views of the surrounding countryside and the historic stone bridge that spans it.

Amphitheater: One of Altos de Chavón's greatest attractions is its spectacular open-air amphitheater, which has held performances by famous performers like as Frank Sinatra, Julio Iglesias, and Sting. Visitors may learn about the history and significance of the amphitheater by exploring its tiered seating, stage, and surrounding gardens.

St. Stanislaus Church: The gorgeous St. Stanislaus Church, a Roman Catholic church, dominates the town skyline and serves as a gathering place for religious and cultural activities. Visitors may take in the church's remarkable architecture, rich craftsmanship, and panoramic views of the surrounding countryside from its hilltop location.

Artisan Workshops: Altos de Chavón is home to a thriving community of artisans and craftsmen who create traditional Dominican handicrafts including ceramics, jewelry, and textiles. Visitors may stroll through the village's lovely cobblestone lanes, stop by local workshops, and buy one-of-a-kind souvenirs to remember their stay.

Regional Museum of Archaeology: The Regional Museum of Archaeology provides insight into the Dominican Republic's pre-Columbian past via artifacts, exhibits, and interactive displays that chronicle the region's indigenous legacy from antiquity to the present.

Tip for the Altos de Chavón Village Tour:

- Wear comfortable walking shoes and light clothing appropriate for exploring cobblestone streets and steep terrain.

- Bring sunscreen, a hat, and lots of drink to keep you hydrated while walking in the sun.

- Take your time soaking up the village's atmosphere, admiring the vistas, and conversing with local artists and inhabitants.

- Consider taking a guided tour lead by skilled local guides who can give information about the village's history, architecture, and cultural significance.

- Bring your camera to capture the beautiful environment and distinctive architectural characteristics of Altos de Chavón.

Overall, the Altos de Chavón Village Tour takes tourists on a compelling trip through time, immersing them in the Dominican Republic's rich history, culture, and natural beauty.

Higuey City Tour.

Higuey, located just a short drive from Punta Cana, is a thriving cultural, commercial, and religious center in the Dominican Republic. With its ancient structures, bustling marketplaces, and colorful street life, Higuey provides tourists with an intriguing peek into Dominican urban life and legacy.

Highlights from the Higuey City Tour:

Basilica of Our Lady of Altagracia: Higuey's main attraction is the majestic Basilica of Our Lady of Altagracia, one of the Dominican Republic's most prominent religious monuments. Built in the 1970s, the basilica is devoted to the Dominican Republic's patron saint and attracts people from all over the world to pay their respects to the Virgin Mary.

Higuey Cathedral: Adjacent to the basilica lies the ancient Higuey Cathedral, a colonial-era cathedral from the 16th century. The cathedral, with its whitewashed walls, beautiful facade, and towering bell towers, is a stunning example of Spanish colonial architecture as well as a symbol of faith and devotion in the local community.

Central Park: Higuey's lively central park serves as a vibrant meeting spot for folks to interact, relax, and enjoy the outdoors. Visitors may wander around the park's lush pathways, observe the colorful flowers and fountains, and enjoy the vibrant ambiance of this bustling urban sanctuary.

Local Markets: Higuey has multiple lively markets and retail areas where tourists may buy a wide range of products, including fresh vegetables, handcrafted crafts, and traditional souvenirs. The Mercado Municipal and Plaza Comercial are popular places to shop, eat, and soak in the bright atmosphere of Higuey's streets.

Historic District: Visitors may see Higuey's colonial-era architecture, which includes attractive pastel-colored houses, elaborate balconies, and cobblestone streets. Highlights include the Casa de la Cultura, a cultural institution situated in a magnificently restored colonial home, and the Fuente de los Leones, a historic fountain with lion statues.

Tips for Higuey City Tour:

- Wear comfortable walking shoes and light attire appropriate for touring metropolitan areas.

- Bring a hat, sunglasses, and sunscreen to protect yourself from the sun's rays when strolling outside.

- Respect local norms and traditions, especially while visiting religious sites and taking part in cultural events.

- Interact with residents, ask questions, and immerse yourself in the colorful street life and culture of Higuey.

- Be aware of your possessions and surroundings, especially in congested locations like markets.

Overall, the Higuey City Tour provides an intriguing look into the history, culture, and daily life of one of the Dominican Republic's most dynamic and colorful cities.

Indigenous Eyes Ecological Park Guided Walk.

The Indigenous Eyes Ecological Park and Reserve, located within the Punta Cana Resort & Club, is a pristine natural refuge where tourists may discover the region's different ecosystems, learn about indigenous culture and traditions, and reconnect with nature.

Highlights from the Indigenous Eyes Ecological Park Guided Walk:

Guided Nature Walk: Led by skilled local guides, visitors may explore the Indigenous Eyes Ecological Park's lush tropical woods, peaceful lagoons, and meandering paths while learning about the region's flora, wildlife, and indigenous legacy. Guides give information on the park's conservation efforts, biological relevance, and cultural significance, enriching the tourist experience and instilling a greater respect for the natural environment.

Freshwater Lagoons: The park has 12 freshwater lagoons known as "eyes" because of their crystal-clear waters and distinctive geological structures. Visitors may take a refreshing plunge in the lagoons, swim among local fish and turtles, or simply rest on the beaches and enjoy the tranquil beauty of these natural sanctuaries.

Interpretive Exhibits: Visitors to the Indigenous Eyes Ecological Park may explore interpretive exhibits and educational displays that give information about the region's indigenous heritage, environmental conservation initiatives, and biodiversity. These displays provide useful information on the park's flora and wildlife, such as native plant species, migrating birds, and endangered animals, as well as the cultural importance of the park's natural resources to the local community.

Birdwatching Opportunities: The park is a birdwatcher's dream, with over 100 species of birds documented within its confines. Guided walks allow you to see colorful tropical birds like parrots, hummingbirds, and herons, as well as migratory species that pass through the region annually. Binoculars and bird identification guides are available to improve the birding experience and assist visitors in identifying the various avian species that inhabit the park.

Cultural Heritage Sites: Visitors may see signs of the region's indigenous Taino heritage throughout the park, such as petroglyphs, ritual sites, and old town ruins. Guided walks emphasize these cultural heritage sites, offering insights into the habits, traditions, and way of life of the indigenous peoples who originally lived in the region. Visitors may learn about the Taino people's profound connection to the land and their sustainable use of natural resources, which will help them appreciate the Dominican Republic's rich cultural legacy even more.

Tip for the Indigenous Eyes Ecological Park Guided Walk:

- Wear comfortable walking shoes and light attire appropriate for outdoor exploring.

- Pack bug repellent, sunscreen, and a reusable water bottle to be comfortable and hydrated on your stroll

- Pay close attention to your guide's explanations and observations, and ask questions to improve your understanding of the park's ecosystem and cultural value.

- Take time to explore the park's natural features, which include lush woods, shimmering lagoons, and a rich range of species.

- Follow the Leave No Trace principles by adhering to park laws and regulations, keeping on designated paths, and limiting your environmental effect.

Overall, the Indigenous Eyes Ecological Park Guided Walk takes guests on a fascinating trip through time and nature, allowing them to connect with the region's indigenous past, discover its different ecosystems, and get a better understanding of the necessity of environmental protection.

Dominican Republic Heritage Tour.

The Dominican Republic Heritage Tour takes tourists on a thorough journey through the country's rich history, culture, and heritage, from pre-Columbian times to colonial legacy and present traditions. Led by professional interpreters, this interactive walking tour takes tourists on a trip through time, stopping at significant historical monuments, cultural icons, and hidden jewels that highlight the varied influences that have molded the Dominican Republic's character.

Highlights from the Dominican Republic Heritage Tour:

Colonial Zone, Santo Domingo: The journey frequently begins at Santo Domingo's colonial zone, which is the Americas' oldest continuously inhabited European settlement and a UNESCO World Heritage site. Visitors may learn about the city's colonial history and architectural legacy by exploring cobblestone streets, ancient plazas, and centuries-old structures like the Alcazar de Colon, the Cathedral of Santa Maria la Menor, and the Ozama Fortress.

Cultural Museums and Art Galleries: Throughout the journey, travelers will have the chance to visit cultural museums, art galleries, and heritage centers that highlight the rich diversity of Dominican culture and artistic expression. Exhibits feature indigenous items, colonial-era artwork, Afro-Caribbean customs, and modern Dominican artists, offering a diverse view of the country's cultural legacy and creative vigor.

Historic sites and Monuments: The trip includes stops at famous sites and monuments that commemorate significant events in Dominican history and honor the country's heroes and cultural icons. Highlights may include the Altar de la Patria, a national mausoleum and monument to the Dominican Republic's founding fathers; the Faro a Colón, a towering lighthouse monument dedicated to Christopher

Columbus; and the Parque Independencia, a public square that represents national pride and unity.

Cultural Performances and Festivals: During the trip, tourists may be able to see live cultural performances, traditional music and dance, and festive festivals that highlight the richness and diversity of Dominican culture. From merengue and bachata performances to Carnival parades and religious festivals, these cultural events shed light on the traditions, practices, and values that determine Dominican identity and communal life.

Tips for The Dominican Republic Heritage Tour:

- Wear comfortable walking shoes and light attire appropriate for touring historic places and metropolitan areas.

- Bring a hat, sunglasses, and sunscreen to protect yourself from the sun's rays when strolling outside.

- Bring a small backpack or bag to carry basics like water, food, and personal items.

- Show respect for local norms and traditions, especially while visiting religious sites and participating in cultural events.

- Meet with local guides, historians, and cultural experts to gain a better grasp of Dominican history, culture, and legacy.

Overall, the Dominican Republic legacy Tour is a fascinating overview of the country's rich and diversified cultural legacy, offering visitors insights into its past, present, and future. From colonial-era sites to modern cultural manifestations, this walking tour provides a complete insight of what makes the Dominican Republic a distinct and exciting destination.

Chapter 14

ITINERARY AND SAMPLE PLANS

Planning a trip to Punta Cana can be both thrilling and frightening, particularly with so many activities and attractions to choose from.

In this chapter, we'll provide two comprehensive sample itineraries to help you make the most of your time in Punta Cana: a Weekend Getaway itinerary for those with limited time, and a Cultural Immersion itinerary for travelers interested in learning more about the region's history, culture, and traditions.

Weekend Getaway Itinerary

For tourists searching for a short trip, Punta Cana is the ideal spot for a weekend of leisure, adventure, and sun. This sample schedule is intended to help you make the most of your weekend and explore everything Punta Cana has to offer.

Day One: Arrival and Beach Relaxation.

Morning:

- Arrive at Punta Cana International Airport, then transport to your hotel or resort.

- Check in, freshen up, and relax into your room.

Afternoon:

- Spend the afternoon at the beach, soaking up the sun, swimming in the blue seas, and participating in water sports like snorkeling, paddleboarding, or kayaking.

Evening:

- Have a great evening at a beachside restaurant, tasting excellent seafood and tropical beverages while watching the sun set over the Caribbean Sea.

- Relax and unwind with a beach bonfire or live music at your resort.

Day Two: Adventure & Exploration.

Morning:

- Begin your day with an adrenaline-pumping experience by ziplining or taking an ATV trip through Punta Cana's gorgeous tropical woods.

- Alternatively, take a catamaran or boat tour to see adjacent islands, snorkel on coral reefs, and swim in hidden lagoons.

Afternoon:

- Have a relaxing lunch at a seaside restaurant, eating typical Dominican cuisine like mofongo, tostones, and fresh ceviche.

- Browse the bright shops, markets, and artisan stalls of Punta Cana Village or Palma Real Shopping Village for souvenirs and gifts to remember your trip.

Evening:

- Take advantage of Punta Cana's active evening by dining and drinking at one of the city's numerous beach bars, nightclubs, or entertainment venues.

- Spend the night dancing to the beats of merengue, bachata, and reggaeton, immersed in the Dominican nightlife scene's irresistible energy and enthusiasm.

Day Three: Relaxation and departure.

Morning:

- Enjoy a leisurely breakfast at your resort, complete with fresh tropical fruits, pastries, and gourmet coffee.

- Take one last walk down the beach, collecting seashells, taking photographs, and enjoying the beauty of your surroundings.

Afternoon:

- In your final hours in Punta Cana, indulge in a peaceful spa treatment or massage, then pamper yourself with premium skincare and wellness routines.

- Check out of your hotel and transport to Punta Cana International Airport for your departing flight, leaving the paradise of Punta Cana with unforgettable memories.

Cultural Immersion Itinerary

For tourists interested in learning more about Punta Cana's history, culture, and legacy, this example itinerary provides a thorough examination of the region's most notable cultural sites, sights, and experiences.

Day One: Arrival and Cultural Exploration

Morning:

- Arrive at Punta Cana International Airport, then transport to your hotel or resort.

- Check in, freshen yourself, and eat a light breakfast before beginning on your cultural journey.

Afternoon:

- Explore Altos de Chavón, a beautifully reproduced 16th-century Mediterranean town, with its cobblestone lanes, artisan workshops, and cultural sites like St. Stanislaus Church and the Regional Museum of Archaeology.

- For lunch, visit one of Altos de Chavón's lovely cafés or restaurants and sample traditional Dominican cuisine while admiring magnificent views of the Chavón River valley.

Evening

- Attend a live concert or cultural event at the Altos de Chavón Amphitheater, where you may see music, dance, and theater productions that highlight Dominican skill and originality.

Day Two: Historical landmarks and heritage sites.

Morning:

- Take a guided tour of Higuey, a thriving city recognized for its historic sites, colonial architecture, and religious significance. Visit the Basilica of Our Lady of Altagracia, the Higuey Cathedral, and Central Park to learn about the city's history, culture, and customs.

Afternoon:

- Wander through Higuey's cobblestone lanes, admire colonial-era architecture, and see cultural landmarks like the Casa de la Cultura and Fuente de los Leones.

- Have lunch at a local restaurant and try regional favorites like sancocho, mangu, and tostones. Pair with cool beverages like morir soñando or mamajuana.

Evening:

- Return to Punta Cana and enjoy the evening immersed in Dominican culture by seeing expert dancers perform merengue, bachata, and other traditional dances.

Day Three: Nature and Heritage.

Morning:

- Take a guided nature walk through Indigenous Eyes Ecological Park and Reserve, discovering lush tropical forests, freshwater lagoons, and cultural heritage sites. Learn about the park's ancient Taino heritage, witness local flora and wildlife, and take in the quiet serenity of nature.

Afternoon:

- Visit the Dominican Republic Heritage Museum or Cultural Center to learn more about the country's history, culture, and identity via interactive exhibitions, multimedia presentations, and educational activities.

- Have a leisurely lunch at a local restaurant while thinking on your cultural immersion experiences and relishing the tastes of Dominican cuisine.

Evening:

- On your final evening in Punta Cana, attend a cultural performance or festival to enjoy Dominican heritage, music, and dance with locals and other guests.

Day Four: Relaxation and departure.

Morning:

- Spend a leisurely morning at your resort, unwinding with a spa treatment, yoga class, or meditation session before you leave.

- Take one last walk along the beach or explore the resort's amenities, taking in the beauty and serenity of your surroundings.

Afternoon:

- Check out of your hotel and transport to Punta Cana International Airport for your departing flight, leaving Punta

Cana's cultural richness and natural beauty with fond memories of an incredible journey.

These example itineraries provide only a taste of the many adventures that await tourists in Punta Cana.

Outdoor Adventure Itinerary

For those who enjoy adrenaline-pumping activities and outdoor exploration, Punta Cana has a multitude of exhilarating excursions nestled among its magnificent natural scenery. This sample itinerary is designed for outdoor enthusiasts who want to enjoy the thrill of ziplining through lush woods, snorkeling in vivid coral reefs, and discovering secret caverns and waterfalls.

Day One: Arrival and Zipline Adventure.

Morning:

- Arrive at Punta Cana International Airport, then transport to your hotel or resort.

- Check in, freshen yourself, and eat a full breakfast to prepare for your day of adventure.

Afternoon:

- Take a thrilling zipline ride across Punta Cana's gorgeous tropical woods. Choose from a variety of zipline routes offered by local adventure businesses, each providing a unique view of the forest canopy and thrilling speeds over the treetops.

- Have lunch at a nearby eco-lodge or adventure park, eating local food while admiring the panoramic views of the surrounding surroundings.

Evening:

- Return to your hotel or resort and rest with a relaxed meal, reflecting on the adrenaline-fueled exploits of the day and planning your outdoor excursions for the following days.

Day Two: Snorkeling and Watersports

Morning:

- Take a guided snorkeling tour to discover the spectacular coral reefs and marine life around Punta Cana's shoreline. Take a catamaran or speedboat to popular snorkeling destinations like the Bavaro Reef or Catalina Island, where you can swim amid colorful fish, sea turtles, and unique coral formations.

- Dive into the crystal-clear waters and immerse yourself in the undersea world, snorkeling with knowledgeable guides who can point out intriguing marine animals and offer safety advice.

Afternoon:

- Enjoy water sports activities like as kayaking, paddleboarding, and windsurfing, taking advantage of Punta Cana's exceptional aquatic conditions. Rent equipment from local beach vendors or join guided excursions led by professional instructors to hone your skills and experience the exhilaration of gliding across the ocean.

- Have a beachside lunch at a seaside restaurant, relishing delicious seafood and tropical beverages while taking in the sun and sea wind.

Evening:

- Spend the evening resting at your hotel or resort, having a leisurely walk along the beach, or taking a sunset cruise down the coast. Relax with a massage or spa treatment to relieve sore muscles and prepare your body for another day of outdoor activities.

Day Three: Cave Exploration and Waterfall Adventure.

Morning:

- Take a guided tour of the Hoyo Azul cave and waterfall, which are located inside the Scape Park in Cap Cana. Hike through lush forests, over suspension bridges, and drop into the depths of the cave, where you'll find a magnificent blue lagoon set among towering limestone walls.

- Take a soothing plunge in Hoyo Azul's cold, clear waters, swimming beneath the gushing waterfall and admiring the natural splendor of this hidden treasure.

Afternoon:

- Continue your outdoor experience with a visit to El Limón Waterfall, a breathtaking natural wonder nestled in the thick woods of the Samaná Peninsula. Hike or ride a horse through the forest to reach the waterfall, then dive into the cool pool below, surrounded by tropical greenery and nature's noises.

- Have a picnic lunch at the base of the waterfall, eating a great meal amidst the breathtaking scenery of the jungle.

Evening:

- Return to Punta Cana and celebrate your outdoor activities with a goodbye meal at a local restaurant, where you can share tales and recollections with other tourists while experiencing the tastes of Dominican cuisine.

Day Four: Relaxation and departure.

Morning:

- Spend a relaxing morning at your hotel or resort, taking a final dip in the pool or strolling along the beach before checking out.

- Pack your bags and prepare to go from Punta Cana, leaving behind memories of exhilarating outdoor excursions and wonderful encounters.

Afternoon:

- Transfer to Punta Cana International Airport for your departing flight, reminiscing on your stay in this tropical paradise and planning your next outdoor adventure.

This outdoor adventure program takes you on an exciting and action-packed tour through Punta Cana's natural treasures, mixing adrenaline-pumping activities with opportunities to reconnect with nature and discover the region's breathtaking surroundings.

Family-Friendly Travel Itinerary

Punta Cana is the ideal place for a fun-filled family holiday, with a diverse choice of activities and attractions for guests of all ages. This example itinerary is designed to give families with a memorable and fun trip to Punta Cana, with beautiful beaches and water parks, as well as engaging wildlife encounters and cultural activities.

Day One: Arrival and Beach Relaxation.

Morning:

- Arrive at Punta Cana International Airport, then transport to your family-friendly resort or hotel.

- Check in, settle into your lodgings, and start your day with a great breakfast.

Afternoon:

- Spend the afternoon with your family at the beach, where you can build sandcastles, swim in the warm Caribbean seas, and soak up some sun.

- Participate in beach games and activities arranged by your resort, such as beach volleyball, sandcastle contests, and kayaking excursions.

Evening:

- Have a family meal at one of the resort's restaurants and try a selection of world cuisines and kid-friendly dishes.

- Enjoy an evening stroll along the beach with your family, collecting seashells and watching the sunset.

Day Two: Water Park Adventure.

Morning:

- Begin your day by visiting a local water park, such as Sirenis Aquagames Punta Cana or Bavaro Adventure Park, which offers a range of exhilarating water slides, lazy rivers, and splash zones.

- Spend the morning splashing and playing in the water park's attractions, getting away from the tropical heat and making unforgettable memories with your family.

Afternoon:

- Have a picnic lunch at the water park or eat at one of the park's onsite restaurants, which provide kid-friendly meals and snacks.

- Continue your water park trip with other rides and attractions, taking stops to rest in the sun and drink cool refreshments.

Evening:

- Return to your hotel or resort and relax with a family movie or game night, where you may watch movies, play board games, or take part in resort-organized entertainment events.

- Have supper at one of the resort's family-friendly restaurants, where you can try a range of delectable cuisine and desserts.

Day Three: Wildlife Encounter and Cultural Experience.

Morning:

- Go on a family-friendly wildlife adventure at Dolphin Island Park or Manati Park Bavaro, where you can interact with dolphins, sea lions, and exotic birds in a safe and instructive setting.

- Engage in hands-on activities like swimming with dolphins, feeding tropical birds, and learning about marine conservation initiatives from professional guides.

Afternoon:

- Immerse your family in the Dominican Republic's rich culture and customs by visiting a local cultural destination like Altos de Chavón Village or Taino Indigenous Village.

- Participate in cultural seminars and activities, such as pottery making, traditional dance lessons, or indigenous artisan presentations, to teach your family about Dominican culture in a fun and participatory setting.

Evening:

- Have a family supper at a traditional Dominican restaurant, where you can try genuine foods like sancocho, tostones, and empanadas.

- Participate in a vibrant cultural presentation or music performance involving traditional Dominican music and dance, which will amuse the entire family.

Day four: Beach day and departure.

Morning:

- Spend your last morning in Punta Cana at the beach with your family. Relax on the sand, swim in the ocean, and engage in beach sports such as beach volleyball, snorkeling, or sandcastle building.

- Take family photographs to capture lasting memories of your time together in paradise.

Afternoon:

- Check out of your hotel or resort and transfer to Punta Cana International Airport to catch your flight.

- Leave Punta Cana with wonderful recollections of your family-friendly holiday, knowing you've had unique adventures and built ties with your loved ones.

This family-friendly schedule strikes the ideal blend of fun, adventure, and leisure, ensuring that each member of the family has a memorable and delightful time in Punta Cana. Punta Cana, with its stunning beaches, interesting activities, and inviting hospitality, is a great place for families looking to make lifetime memories together.

Budget Travel Itinerary

Traveling on a budget does not mean losing fun and adventure, especially in a place like Punta Cana, where there are several economical activities and lodgings to choose from. This sample schedule is intended to help budget-conscious tourists make the most of their stay in Punta Cana without breaking the bank.

Day One: Arrival, Beach Exploration

Morning:

- Arrive at Punta Cana International Airport and transport to your affordable lodging, such as a hostel, guesthouse, or budget hotel.

- Check in, drop off your things, and have a quick breakfast at a nearby café or bakery.

Afternoon:

- Spend the afternoon at the beach, exploring the coastline and enjoying free activities like swimming, sunbathing, and beachcombing.

- Bring your own snacks and drinks to the beach to save money on food and beverages, or hunt for economical beachside eateries and food vendors with low-cost alternatives.

Evening:

- Make a modest meal at your lodging with supplies acquired from a nearby supermarket or convenience shop.

- Take a leisurely stroll down the beach at sunset, appreciating the breathtaking vistas and taking in the laid-back attitude of Punta Cana's coastline.

Day Two: Outdoor Adventures on a Budget

Morning:

- Begin your day with a trek or nature walk in a nearby park or reserve, such as Indigenous Eyes Ecological Park, which has free or low-cost admission for guests.

- Walk the park's trails, lagoons, and animal observation places to appreciate the natural splendor of Punta Cana's sceneries without spending a fortune.

Afternoon:

- Pack a picnic lunch and head to Macao Beach, a favorite destination for budget visitors seeking a day of sun, sand, and surf.

- Spend the afternoon swimming, surfing, or simply lounging on the beach, taking advantage of the complimentary facilities and natural beauty of this magnificent coastline.

Evening:

- Return to your lodging and prepare supper with inexpensive items from a nearby market or grocery shop.

- Meet other budget travelers at your hotel or neighboring hostels and share ideas, stories, and recommendations for enjoying Punta Cana on a budget.

Day Three: Cultural Immersion on a Budget.

Morning:

- Shop at a local or artisan market for souvenirs, gifts, and handicrafts created by local craftsmen. Look for inexpensive souvenirs like handcrafted jewelry, fabrics, and artwork.

Afternoon:

- Visit Punta Cana's cultural attractions for free or at a reasonable cost, including museums, galleries, and history sites. Visit the Altos de Chavón hamlet, a reconstructed 16th-century Mediterranean hamlet with free access to its cobblestone streets, shops, and galleries.

Evening:

- Have a low-cost meal at a neighborhood restaurant or food stand while enjoying classic Dominican street cuisine like empanadas, tostones, and pastelitos.

- Finish your evening with a stroll along the Malecón, or waterfront promenade, where you can enjoy free entertainment including street performers, live music, and cultural activities.

Day Four: Departures and Reflections

Morning:

- Have one last breakfast at a low-cost café or bakery, relishing the tastes of Dominican coffee and pastries.

- Check out of your hotel and transfer to Punta Cana International Airport for your trip home, reflecting on your low-cost travel adventures and Punta Cana vacation memories.

Afternoon:

- Say goodbye to Punta Cana with gratitude for the inexpensive adventures, cultural discoveries, and unique experiences you had throughout your budget-friendly vacation.

- Leave Punta Cana feeling accomplished and satisfied, knowing that you made the most of your stay in this tropical paradise without overpaying.

This budget vacation plan proves that you may enjoy the beauty and excitement of Punta Cana without breaking the bank. Budget travelers may have a rewarding and memorable journey to this Caribbean jewel with careful preparation, shrewd spending, and a sense of adventure.

Solo Traveler's Guide

Solo travel to Punta Cana provides a unique opportunity for self-discovery, adventure, and relaxation in a breathtaking tropical paradise. This solo traveler's guide offers advice and ideas for anyone wishing to explore Punta Cana alone and make the most of their solo trip.

Day One: Arrival and Solo Exploration

Morning:

- Arrive at Punta Cana International Airport and transfer to your accommodation, which might be a hostel, guesthouse, or solo-friendly hotel.

- Check in, drop off your things, and spend some time getting acquainted with your surroundings and the facilities of your lodging.

Afternoon:

- Set out to explore Punta Cana's beaches, beginning with Bavaro Beach, one of the most popular and scenic in the area.

- Relax in a beach chair or blanket, enjoy the sun, and cool down in the Caribbean Sea's beautiful waves.

Evening:

- Have supper at a beachfront restaurant, relishing excellent seafood and tropical beverages while you watch the sunset over the water.

- After supper, take a leisurely stroll down the beach, admiring the peace and beauty of the nocturnal shoreline.

Day Two: Adventure & Excursions.

Morning:

- Take an adventure journey to discover Punta Cana's natural beauty and adrenaline-pumping activities. Ziplining through the forest, horseback riding on the beach, and discovering secret caverns and waterfalls are all options.

Afternoon:

- Take a group trip or excursion to meet other tourists and share your experiences while visiting Punta Cana's attractions. Discover the Caribbean Sea's underwater delights with activities such as snorkeling, scuba diving, or catamaran sailing.

Evening:

- Meet other single travelers at your hotel or a nearby bar, and share tales, ideas, and recommendations for visiting Punta Cana.

- Spend the night out with new acquaintances, discovering Punta Cana's nightlife scene and taking in the city's dynamic atmosphere after dark.

Day Three: Cultural immersion and relaxation.

Morning:

- Immerse yourself in Punta Cana's history and tradition by visiting Altos de Chavón, a reconstructed 16th-century Mediterranean hamlet with cobblestone alleys, artisan workshops, and cultural attractions.

Afternoon:

- Spend the day visiting Punta Cana's cultural sites and attractions, such as the Basilica of Our Lady of Altagracia or the Indigenous Eyes Ecological Park and Reserve, to learn about the region's indigenous legacy and environmental conservation efforts.

Evening:

- Treat yourself to a solitary evening at a local restaurant, where you may experience wonderful Dominican cuisine and Caribbean spices.

- Reflect on your solo travel experiences and activities in Punta Cana by journaling or photographing memories to treasure for years to come.

Day Four: Departures and Reflections

Morning:

- Have one last breakfast in Punta Cana, maybe at a café or bakery you've been meaning to sample during your stay.

- Take a final stroll along the beach or through Punta Cana's streets, taking in the sights and sounds of the colorful city before leaving.

Afternoon:

- Check out of your hotel and transfer to Punta Cana International Airport for your departing flight.

- Reflect on your solo travel experience in Punta Cana, valuing the moments of self-discovery, adventure, and relaxation you had throughout your stay in this tropical paradise.

Departure:

- Say goodbye to Punta Cana, grateful for the memories and experiences you earned on your single voyage.

- Board your aircraft home or on to your next destination, bringing with you the lessons learnt and confidence acquired by traveling alone in one of the Caribbean's most beautiful locations.

This solo traveler's guide to Punta Cana provides a road map for solitary explorers wishing to explore the area alone and make the most of their solo trip. Punta Cana's beautiful beaches, fascinating activities, and inviting hospitality make it an ideal destination for single travelers seeking adventure, relaxation, and self-discovery.

Romantic Getaways in Punta Cana.

Punta Cana, with its stunning beaches, turquoise ocean, and opulent resorts, is an excellent choice for romantic getaways.

This romantic holiday plan is intended to help couples make amazing memories and reconnect in the breathtaking environment of Punta Cana.

Day One: Arrival and Relaxation

Morning:

- Arrive at Punta Cana International Airport, then transport to your romantic resort or boutique hotel.

- Check in and relax after your travel, sipping a welcome drink and taking in the tropical environment of your accommodations.

Afternoon:

- Spend the afternoon resting by the pool or on the beach, absorbing in the warm Caribbean sun and enjoying one another's company.

- Treat yourself to a couples' massage or spa treatment at the resort's spa, where you may indulge in exquisite treatments and revitalizing cures.

Evening:

- Have a romantic candlelit supper at one of Punta Cana's luxury restaurants, where you can appreciate gourmet cuisine and superb wines while taking in the stunning views of the ocean.

- Toast to your love and the beginning of your romantic holiday beneath the starry night sky, cherishing every minute together in this tropical paradise.

Day Two: Private excursion and adventure.

Morning:

- Begin your day with a private trip for two, such as a private catamaran sail, helicopter tour, or beachside horseback riding expedition.

- Enjoy the exclusivity and intimacy of your private adventure as you discover Punta Cana's natural beauty and beautiful surroundings together.

Afternoon:

- Have a romantic picnic lunch on a quiet beach or gorgeous vantage point, where you can enjoy each other's company while admiring nature's beauty.

- Take advantage of the opportunity to engage in water sports such as snorkeling, paddleboarding, or swimming in quiet coves and crystal blue lagoons.

Evening:

- Return to your lodging and clean up before a romantic evening out on the town.

- Dine at a seaside restaurant and enjoy fresh seafood and unique beverages while listening to the waves smashing against the coast.

Day Three: Sunset Romance and Fine Dining.

Morning:

- Have a relaxing breakfast in bed or in a comfortable café, savoring delectable pastries, tropical fruits, and freshly made coffee.

Afternoon:

- Spend the afternoon on a sunset boat down the shore to see Punta Cana's romantic side. Sail into the golden hues of the sunset, drinking champagne and spending private moments as you float across the sea.

- Capture the joy of the moment with images and memories you'll have for a lifetime.

Evening:

- End your romantic weekend with a gourmet dinner experience at a top-rated restaurant, complete with a multi-course tasting menu matched with premium wines.

- Toast to your love and the beautiful memories you've made throughout your romantic holiday in Punta Cana, relishing every moment together in this tropical paradise.

Day Four: Departures and Reflections

Morning:

- Have a leisurely breakfast together while reminiscing about your romantic holiday and reliving your best memories.

- Take a final walk down the beach, holding hands and admiring the beauty of the ocean before saying farewell to Punta Cana.

Afternoon:

- Check out of your hotel and transfer to Punta Cana International Airport for your departing flight.

- Depart Punta Cana with hearts full of love and memories of a really amazing romantic weekend to one of the Caribbean's most beautiful places.

This romantic holiday itinerary provides couples with the ideal balance of leisure, adventure, and romance in the breathtaking backdrop of Punta Cana.

Chapter 15

SUSTAINABLE TOURISM PRACTICES IN PUNTA CANA.

Punta Cana, known for its beautiful beaches, crystal-clear oceans, and active culture, has become a favorite resort for those seeking sun, sand, and relaxation. However, as tourism grows, it is critical to promote sustainable practices to protect the region's natural beauty and cultural history for future generations.

In this chapter, we'll look at Punta Cana's sustainable tourism practices, with a focus on eco-friendly accommodations, responsible wildlife tourism, community assistance, and Leave No Trace principles.

Environmentally Friendly Resorts and Accommodations

The implementation of eco-friendly techniques by resorts and lodging providers is a key component of Punta Cana's sustainable tourism strategy. Many establishments in the region have adopted sustainability efforts to reduce their environmental effect and encourage responsible tourism. The following are some essential elements of eco-friendly resorts and accommodations:

Energy Efficiency: Eco-friendly resorts promote energy efficiency by utilizing renewable energy sources, installing energy-saving appliances and lights, and adopting smart energy management systems to cut power use.

Water Conservation: Water shortage is a major problem for many tourist areas, including Punta Cana. Eco-friendly resorts tackle this problem by introducing water-saving technology including low-flow faucets and toilets, rainwater harvesting systems, and water reuse/recycling programs.

Waste Management: Proper waste management is critical for lowering pollution and protecting natural ecosystems. Eco-friendly Punta Cana resorts conduct waste reduction and recycling programs, compost organic waste, and reduce single-use plastics through efforts such as distributing reusable water bottles and removing plastic straws.

Sustainable Architecture and Design: Many eco-friendly resorts in Punta Cana incorporate sustainable design principles into their architecture and construction, such as using locally sourced materials, optimizing natural ventilation and daylighting, and using low-impact construction techniques to reduce environmental impact.

Environmental Education and Awareness: Eco-friendly resorts provide visitors with environmental education and awareness programs such as guided nature walks, eco-tours, and sustainability seminars to create knowledge about local ecosystems, wildlife protection, and sustainable living practices.

Choosing eco-friendly resorts and accommodations in Punta Cana allows guests to reduce their environmental impact while also supporting sustainable tourism projects that help local people and ecosystems.

Responsible Wildlife Tourism.

Responsible wildlife tourism is another important component of sustainable tourism in Punta Cana, allowing visitors to watch and engage with native animals while limiting detrimental impacts on animal welfare and natural environments. Here are some guidelines for ethical wildlife tourism:

Respect Wildlife: Responsible visitors to Punta Cana should observe animals from a safe distance, avoid feeding or touching them, and avoid engaging in activities that disrupt their natural habits or habitats.

Choose Ethical Tour Operators: When booking wildlife tours or excursions, tourists should look for reputable tour operators who value animal care, adhere to ethical norms, and support conservation efforts. Look for operators who have been accredited by recognized organizations such as the Global Sustainable Tourism Council (GSTC) or are linked with credible conservation non-governmental organizations (NGOs).

Avoid Captive Animal Attractions: Punta Cana, like many other tourist locations, includes attractions that involve captive animals, such as dolphin encounters, animal shows, and petting zoos. Responsible tourists should avoid supporting these activities, which frequently include the exploitation and maltreatment of animals for entertainment purposes.

Support Conservation Efforts: Travelers may help wildlife conservation in Punta Cana by donating to respected conservation groups and programs that conserve endangered species, maintain natural ecosystems, and encourage sustainable wildlife tourism. Consider giving to local conservation organizations, volunteering for wildlife research or rehabilitation programs, or taking part in eco-tours that benefit conservation efforts.

By practicing responsible wildlife tourism, visitors may have meaningful wildlife encounters in Punta Cana while also protecting and preserving native ecosystems and animal populations for future generations.

Supporting Local Communities

Supporting local communities is an essential component of sustainable tourism in Punta Cana, where tourism not only benefits the economy but also has social and cultural consequences for the locals. Here are some ways that tourists may help local communities:

Choose Locally Owned Businesses: When looking for lodgings, eating options, and tour operators in Punta Cana, choose locally owned and run businesses that reinvest earnings back into the community, provide job opportunities for locals, and contribute to the local economy.

Buy Locally Made goods: Help local artisans and craftsmen by purchasing souvenirs, handicrafts, and goods that celebrate Dominican culture and heritage. Look for artisan markets, craft fairs, and cooperatives where you may purchase handcrafted items directly from local craftspeople.

Learn About Local Culture: Learn about Dominican culture, traditions, and customs by engaging in cultural activities, attending festivals and events, and mingling with locals. Respect local customs and manners, and look for ways to interact with communities in a respectful and meaningful way.

Give Back Through Volunteering: Consider giving your time and skills to help with community development projects, educational initiatives, or environmental conservation activities in Punta Cana. Many non-governmental organizations (NGOs) seek volunteers to help with activities including beach cleanups, community gardening, and youth outreach initiatives.

Supporting local communities in Punta Cana allows travelers to contribute to long-term development, stimulate cultural interaction, and produce good social consequences that benefit both inhabitants and visitors.

Leave No Trace Principles.

Leave No Trace (LNT) is an outdoor ethics program that encourages ethical conduct and minimum damage on natural surroundings. These concepts are critical to maintaining the unspoiled beauty of Punta Cana's beaches, forests, and marine habitats. Here are the Leave No Trace principles and how they relate to sustainable tourism in Punta Cana:

Plan Ahead and Prepare: Before visiting Punta Cana, look into local rules, cultural norms, and environmental conditions to ensure you're ready for safe outdoor activities. Pack basic supplies like as water, food, sunscreen, and bug repellent, and plan environmentally friendly activities.

Travel and Camp on Durable Surfaces: When visiting Punta Cana's natural regions, stay on approved trails, beaches, and campsites to prevent harming sensitive ecosystems and habitats. Avoid trampling plants, upsetting wildlife, or establishing new trails that might cause erosion and habitat degradation.

Proper Waste Disposal: Separate all garbage and recyclables, including cigarette butts, food scraps, and packaging. To leave the environment cleaner than you found it, use designated garbage and recycling bins wherever available, and pack out whatever you bring into natural areas.

Leave What You Find: Respect Punta Cana's natural beauty and cultural legacy by leaving natural and cultural objects intact. Avoid picking flowers, collecting shells, or removing rocks, plants, or artifacts from their native habitats, as these activities can harm ecosystems and cultural heritage.

Minimize Campfire Impacts: If camping in Punta Cana, use existing fire rings or authorized fire pits to reduce the environmental effect of campfires. To avoid wildfires and environmental damage, keep fires small, fuel them exclusively with dead and fell wood, and totally extinguish them before leaving.

Respect Wildlife: Keep a safe distance from wildlife and avoid approaching or disturbing it in its natural habitat. Never feed wild animals or try to entice them with food, as this might disturb their normal behavior and lead to a reliance on human handouts.

Be Respectful to Other guests: Show kindness and concern to other guests, locals, and wildlife in Punta Cana by reducing noise, respecting privacy, and sharing public places responsibly. Yield to others on paths and beaches, keep dogs under control, and avoid behaviors that may disrupt or inconvenience others.

By following the Leave No Trace principles, visitors may reduce their environmental effect and help maintain the natural beauty and biological integrity of Punta Cana's landscapes for future generations to enjoy.

To summarize, sustainable tourism practices are critical to sustaining Punta Cana's long-term profitability and resilience as a top tourist destination. Travelers can help preserve Punta Cana's natural and cultural heritage while having meaningful and authentic travel experiences by choosing eco-friendly accommodations, practicing responsible wildlife tourism, supporting local communities, and adhering to Leave No Trace principles. We can encourage sustainable tourism in Punta Cana and create a more sustainable future for this lovely Caribbean destination by working together and taking individual responsibility.

Chapter 16

SAFETY TIPS AND EMERGENCY INFORMATION.

Safety is a primary consideration for visitors to any resort, especially Punta Cana. While Punta Cana is usually regarded as a safe tourist location, it is critical to be aware of possible hazards and take steps to guarantee a safe and pleasurable vacation.

In this chapter, we'll go over safety recommendations and emergency information to assist tourists be aware and prepared when visiting Punta Cana.

Healthcare and Medical Services

Maintaining good health and getting medical care are critical components of remaining safe when visiting Punta Cana. Here's some health and medical advice for travelers:

Travel Health Insurance: Before heading to Punta Cana, make sure you have comprehensive travel health insurance that covers medical emergencies, hospitals, and medical evacuations. Check coverage for water sports, adventurous activities, and pre-existing medical problems.

Vaccinations and Health Precautions: Consult your doctor or travel clinic to see if any vaccinations or health precautions are required for travel to Punta Cana. Common recommendations include hepatitis A and typhoid immunizations, as well as protection against mosquito-borne diseases including dengue fever and Zika virus.

Sun Safety: To protect yourself from the sun's damaging rays, apply sunscreen with a high SPF, seek shade during peak hours, and wear protective clothing such hats, sunglasses, and lightweight long-sleeved shirts. Stay hydrated by drinking lots of water, especially during hot and humid conditions.

Food and Water Safety: To avoid foodborne diseases, select reputed restaurants and food vendors with high cleanliness standards. Avoid drinking tap water, ice cubes, and raw or undercooked meals, as they may be contaminated. Stick to bottled water and drinks in sealed containers.

Medical Facilities: Learn about the locations of Punta Cana's medical facilities, hospitals, and pharmacies. Major resorts and tourist destinations frequently provide on-site medical facilities or access to neighboring medical services. In the event of a medical emergency, contact your accommodation's front desk or seek help from local authorities.

Emergency Contacts.

It is critical to understand how to get help and support when in Punta Cana in the event of an emergency. Here are some vital emergency contact details for travelers:

Emergency Services: Call 911 for quick help in case of an accident, medical emergency, or criminal event. The emergency services dispatcher will link you with the proper authorities, such as police, firefighters, or medical personnel.

Tourist Police: Punta Cana has a specific Tourist Police team that assists tourists and visitors. Tourist Police can assist with lost things, small disagreements, and other non-emergency situations involving tourists. Contact the Tourist Police at 809-552-1757.

Embassy or Consulate: If you are a foreign traveler and need assistance from your country's embassy or consulate, contact the nearest diplomatic post for advice and support. Keep a copy of your passport and embassy contact information in a secure and easily accessible area when abroad.

Crime and Personal Safety.

While Punta Cana is mostly secure for tourists, you must be careful and take steps to safeguard yourself and your things. Here are some crime prevention and personal safety suggestions for travelers:

Protect your valuables: While touring Punta Cana, keep passports, cash, credit cards, and other gadgets secure and out of sight. When not in use, store valuables in hotel safes or with secure locks, and avoid carrying large sums of cash or wearing costly jewelry in public.

Be Aware of Your Surroundings: If you feel uncomfortable or dangerous in a specific place, heed your instincts. Avoid going alone in poorly lit or secluded regions, particularly at night, and instead stick to densely populated and well-lighted areas wherever feasible.

Choose Reliable Transportation: When visiting Punta Cana, choose trustworthy transportation options like as licensed taxis, hotel shuttles, or ride-sharing applications. Avoid unregistered or unofficial transportation providers, especially late at night, and check vehicle safety and driver credentials before entering a vehicle.

Avoid Excessive Alcohol Intake: While it may be tempting to indulge in tropical drinks and beverages while in Punta

Cana, limit your alcohol intake, especially in new or unsupervised surroundings. Drink wisely, pace yourself, and know your limitations to prevent being a victim of crime or an accident.

Be Wary of frauds: Be wary of popular tourist frauds, such as bogus tour operators, timeshare presentations, and street hustlers that offer unwanted services or items. Before dealing with new people or firms, use caution and conduct comprehensive investigation.

Cultural Sensitivity and Respectable Behavior

Respecting local customs, traditions, and cultural norms is critical for building strong relationships with people and having a wonderful and respectful vacation in Punta Cana. Here are some cultural-sensitive and polite conduct suggestions for travelers:

Dress appropriately: When visiting religious institutions, cultural landmarks, or local communities in Punta Cana, please dress modestly and politely. Avoid wearing exposing clothing or apparel that might be deemed unpleasant or improper in conservative surroundings.

Learn simple Spanish words: While English is frequently spoken in Punta Cana's tourist districts, learning simple Spanish words like hello, thank you, and please will help you communicate more effectively and show respect for the local language and culture.

Ask Permission Before Photographing Always get permission before photographing persons, particularly locals and indigenous cultures. Respect privacy and cultural sensitivity when photographing, and avoid intruding on private locations or rituals unless explicitly permitted.

Respect Local Customs and Traditions: Learn about Dominican customs, traditions, and social etiquette to prevent offending or misunderstanding others. Respect religious rites, cultural customs, and social conventions, and seek advice from locals or tour guides if you are confused about proper behavior.

Support Local Communities: Buy locally manufactured items, take part in community-based tourist experiences, and respect indigenous land rights and sovereignty to help local artisans, businesses, and cultural activities thrive. Contribute favorably to the local economy while also showing admiration for Dominican culture and tradition.

Travelers who practice cultural awareness and courteous behavior may generate pleasant cross-cultural encounters, promote mutual understanding, and help to preserve Punta Cana's cultural legacy and character.

To summarize, safety is crucial for visitors to Punta Cana, and being aware and prepared is critical to ensuring a safe and pleasurable experience. Travelers may stay safe and enjoy their time in this lovely Caribbean resort by following health and medical recommendations, having emergency contact information, adopting crime prevention procedures, and respecting local customs and culture. With caution, common sense, and respect, visitors may enjoy all that Punta Cana has to offer while emphasizing their safety and well-being.

Chapter 17

ACCESSIBILITY AT PUNTA CANA.

Accessibility is an important component of travel for people with disabilities, ensuring that everyone can discover and enjoy the attractions of Punta Cana.

In this chapter, we will look at the accessibility alternatives available in Punta Cana, including as accessible lodging and transportation, wheelchair-friendly attractions and facilities, help services for disabled people, and inclusive activities.

Accessible Accommodation and Transportation

Ensuring accessible accommodation and transportation alternatives is critical for disabled guests to have a comfortable and hassle-free stay in Punta Cana. Here are some considerations for accessible housing and transportation:

Accessible Accommodation: Many hotels and resorts in Punta Cana have accessible rooms and services for visitors with mobility limitations. Accessible rooms may have larger entrances, roll-in showers, grab bars, and other accessible amenities to guarantee a comfortable stay for disabled visitors. When reserving accommodations, be sure to ask about accessible room options and special accessibility amenities.

Transportation Options: Travelers with disabilities need accessible transportation to get about Punta Cana and its surroundings. While public transportation in Punta Cana may be limited in accessibility, tourists with mobility impairments may be able to use private transportation services such as accessible taxis or rental vehicles equipped with wheelchair ramps or lifts. Additionally, several hotels and resorts provide accessible shuttle services for visitors with impairments.

Wheelchair-Friendly Attractions and Facilities.

Punta Cana has a number of wheelchair-accessible attractions and amenities, allowing those with disabilities to enjoy the destination's natural beauty and cultural attractions. Here are some wheelchair-accessible attractions and amenities in Punta Cana:

Beach Access: Many beaches in Punta Cana have wheelchair-accessible walkways and ramps to help those with disabilities get to the coastline and shoreline. Beach wheelchairs with bigger tires may also be supplied at some resorts or rental facilities so that visitors with mobility problems can enjoy beach activities.

Accessible Excursions: Several tour companies in Punta Cana provide accessible excursions and activities for guests with impairments. Accessible tours might include sightseeing excursions, boat cruises, and cultural activities that promote accessibility and inclusion for all participants.

Wheelchair-Friendly Facilities: Major tourist destinations, such as shopping malls, restaurants, and entertainment venues, frequently have wheelchair-accessible toilets, ramps, elevators, and designated parking places. These facilities are intended to provide equal access and convenience for guests with impairments.

Support Services for Visitors with Disabilities

Punta Cana provides assistance services and resources to travelers with impairments, ensuring a smooth vacation experience. Here are some help services for guests with disabilities:

Accessibility Information: Many tourism websites, visitor centers, and lodging providers in Punta Cana give accessibility information and assistance to visitors with disabilities. Accessibility guides, maps, and brochures may provide information on accessible attractions, amenities, and modes of transportation to assist guests in planning their trip.

Personal Assistance Services: Some Punta Cana hotels and resorts provide personal assistance services to disabled visitors, such as mobility aids, personal care support, and accessible equipment rental. Travelers can inquire about these services while reserving accommodations to ensure that their individual requirements are addressed throughout their stay.

Medical and Emergency Assistance: Access to medical and emergency services is critical for disabled travelers in the event of unforeseen health problems or crises. Punta Cana includes medical facilities, hospitals, and emergency services that can help tourists with impairments. Travelers should bring any essential medical information, medicines, and emergency contacts with them on their journey.

Inclusionary Activities and Events

Inclusive programs and events are critical for ensuring that people with disabilities have full access to Punta Cana's cultural and recreational offerings. Here are some inclusive activities and events for tourists with disabilities:

Adaptive Sports and Recreation: Punta Cana provides chances for adaptive sports and recreational activities geared for those with impairments. Adaptive water activities, such as adaptive snorkeling, scuba diving, and kayaking, allow those with mobility limitations to enjoy the beauty of Punta Cana's marine settings.

Cultural Performances and Events: Punta Cana's cultural performances, music festivals, and special events may include accommodations for people with disabilities, such as reserved seats, accessible viewing places, and sign language interpretation. Travelers should ask about accessibility adjustments when visiting cultural events to guarantee a good and inclusive experience.

Accessible Dining and Entertainment: Many restaurants, bars, and entertainment venues in Punta Cana provide wheelchair-accessible doors, tables, and seating sections. Inclusive eating and entertainment choices enable those with disabilities to experience Punta Cana's dynamic culinary and nightlife scene alongside their fellow guests.

Punta Cana strives to provide an inclusive and friendly atmosphere for guests of all abilities by prioritizing accessibility in accommodations, transportation, attractions, and services. Individuals with disabilities may confidently and easily explore and enjoy the beauty and diversity of Punta Cana thanks to its accessible facilities, help services, and inclusive activities.

Help improve the color, contrast, sharpness, and other characteristics of your photographs while keeping a natural and genuine appearance.

Adjust Exposure and Contrast: Begin by altering the exposure and contrast to ensure that your images have balanced lighting and dynamic range. Use the exposure and contrast sliders to brighten shadows, darken highlights, and increase overall contrast to create a more visually attractive image.

Fine-Tune Color and White Balance: Adjust the temperature and tint sliders to produce accurate and natural-looking colors. Experiment with saturation and vibrance changes to boost or tone down colors while retaining skin tones and other vital components.

Crop and Straighten: Crop and straighten your photographs to improve composition and eliminate distracting things from the frame. Cropping tools may be used to change the aspect ratio, composition, and frame of a photo to make it look more appealing.

Sharpen and Reduce Noise: Use sharpening and noise reduction to improve image clarity and detail while reducing digital noise and artifacts. Sharpening sliders may be used to improve edge definition, and noise reduction settings can be fine-tuned to retain picture quality, particularly in low-light or high-ISO scenarios.

Experiment with Creative Effects: To add artistic flare to your images, try using vignetting, selective color tweaks, and graded filters. Use presets or custom modifications to create distinct appearances and styles that represent your creative vision.

Share your images: Once you've finished editing your images to your liking, it's time to show them off to the world. Consider sharing your photographs on social media sites like Instagram, Facebook, and Twitter to promote your photography and encourage people to visit Punta Cana. Use relevant hashtags, geotags, and descriptions to boost the exposure and engagement of your images.

Print and Display: By printing your best images from your Punta Cana trip, you can enjoy them in real form while also sharing them with friends and family. Consider producing picture albums, framed prints, or canvas prints to display your memories and relive your Punta Cana adventures.

By following these editing and sharing suggestions, you may improve the visual impact of your trip photographs and create lasting memories of your time in Punta Cana.

To summarize, photography is an effective technique for capturing the beauty and soul of Punta Cana, allowing visitors to save their memories and share their experiences with others. Explore the best photography spots, capture the essence of the destination, master smartphone and DSLR photography techniques, and edit and share your travel photos to create stunning images that will showcase Punta Cana's natural beauty, vibrant culture, and unique charm for years to come.

Chapter 18

PHOTO GUIDE TO PUNTA CANA

Photography is an effective approach to capture the beauty and character of Punta Cana, a tropical paradise noted for its pristine beaches, blue oceans, and colorful culture.

In this chapter, we'll look at the greatest photography places in Punta Cana, how to capture the spirit of the destination, smartphone and DSLR shooting techniques, and ways to edit and share your trip images.

Top Photography Spots

Punta Cana has a variety of gorgeous settings ideal for taking amazing shots. From beautiful beaches to lush scenery, here are some of the top shooting places in Punta Cana:

Bavaro Beach: With its pristine white sand and crystal-clear seas, Bavaro Beach is one of Punta Cana's most picturesque sites. Capture sweeping vistas of the coastline, vivid sunsets, and beachgoers engaged in water sports like swimming, snorkeling, and sunbathing.

Macao Beach: Macao Beach is popular among photographers due to its natural beauty and rustic appeal. Photographers may photograph spectacular seascapes, breaking waves, and local fisherman at work on the coast. Don't pass up the opportunity to shoot surfers surfing the waves at this renowned surf site.

Hoyo Azul: Hoyo Azul, often known as Blue Hole, is a hidden gem situated deep in the Dominican jungle. This natural cenote has magnificent blue waters surrounded by dense flora, providing a magical setting for photography. Capture the vivid hues and distinct charm of this natural treasure.

Indigenous Eyes Ecological Park: Explore the park's lush landscapes and various ecosystems, which include 12 freshwater lagoons and miles of picturesque pathways. Wander through the park's tranquil settings and photograph natural flora and animals, such as unusual birds, butterflies, and tropical plants.

Altos de Chavón: Travel back in time and experience the old-world elegance of Altos de Chavón, a reconstructed 16th-century Mediterranean town set atop a hill overlooking the Chavón River. This unique cultural site provides opportunities to photograph cobblestone streets, old architecture, and panoramic vistas of the surrounding countryside.

Catching the Essence of Punta Cana

To capture the spirit of Punta Cana in your images, emphasize the destination's natural beauty, colorful culture, and relaxed attitude. Here are some suggestions for capturing the essence of Punta Cana in your photographs:

Embrace Natural Light: Punta Cana is blessed with plenty of sunshine and beautiful natural light, making it excellent for photography. Use golden hour lighting at dawn and sunset to capture soft, warm tones and dramatic shadows that highlight the beauty of the countryside.

Include Local Culture: Incorporate elements of Dominican culture and daily life into your images to create a more full picture of Punta Cana. Capture street scenes, vibrant marketplaces, classic buildings, and local craftspeople in action to highlight the destination's rich cultural legacy.

Capture Authentic Moments: Look for genuine moments and honest emotions that embody the essence of Punta Cana. Look for authentic moments that show the excitement and vibrancy of life in Punta Cana, such as a family playing on the beach, people dancing to merengue music, or fisherman pulling in their catch of the day.

Venture off the Beaten Path: Go beyond the tourist destinations and find Punta Cana's hidden beauties and lesser-known areas for one-of-a-kind photo possibilities. Exploring off the beaten route, whether it's a lonely beach, a peaceful forest sanctuary, or a picturesque hamlet, may result in unique shooting experiences.

Tips for Smartphone and DSLR Photography.

Whether you're using a smartphone or a DSLR camera, there are ways to take amazing images in Punta Cana. Here are some suggestions for DSLR and smartphone photography:

Smartphone Photography:

Use HDR option: The HDR (High Dynamic Range) option allows you to shoot well-exposed images in high-contrast lighting circumstances, such as bright sunshine or shaded regions. Enable HDR mode on your smartphone to get balanced exposure and rich colors in your images.

Experiment with Composition: Use the rule of thirds, leading lines, and framing strategies to create visually pleasing smartphone photographs. Experiment with various angles and perspectives to create dynamic compositions that draw the viewer's attention to the scene.

Edit with Mobile tools: Use mobile editing tools like Adobe Lightroom, Snapseed, and VSCO to improve your smartphone images. To achieve professional-quality results, fine-tune your photographs' exposure, contrast, saturation, and other factors.

DSLR Photography:

Use Manual Mode: Shooting in manual mode allows you to modify aperture, shutter speed, and ISO for the best exposure and creative flexibility. To obtain the desired appearance, use several settings such as narrow depth of focus for blurred backgrounds and long exposures for silky smooth water effects.

Use Filters and Accessories: Enhance your DSLR pictures using polarizing filters, neutral density filters, and tripod mounts. Filters may assist minimize glare, improve colors, and produce artistic effects, whilst a tripod offers steadiness for long exposures and low-light photography.

Shoot in RAW Format: Instead of JPEG, capture photographs in RAW format for the best image quality and editing versatility. RAW files include more image data and provide you more control over post-processing, such as exposure, white balance, and color correction.

Editing and Sharing your Travel Photos

After taking your photographs in Punta Cana, editing and sharing them helps you to increase their visual impact while also sharing your experiences with others. Here are some suggestions for editing and sharing your vacation photographs:

Choose the Right Editing program: Choose a picture editing program that is appropriate for your skill level and editing requirements. Adobe Lightroom, Photoshop, and Capture One are popular solutions for processing trip images. Experiment with various editing tools and techniques to improve the color, contrast, sharpness, and other characteristics of your images while keeping a natural and genuine appearance.

Adjust Exposure and Contrast: Begin by altering the exposure and contrast to ensure that your images have balanced lighting and dynamic range. Use the exposure and contrast sliders to brighten shadows, darken highlights, and increase overall contrast to create a more visually attractive image.

Fine-Tune Color and White Balance: Adjust the temperature and tint sliders to produce accurate and natural-looking colors. Experiment with saturation and vibrance changes to boost or tone down colors while retaining skin tones and other vital components.

Crop and Straighten: Crop and straighten your photographs to improve composition and eliminate distracting things from the frame. Cropping tools may be used to change the aspect ratio, composition, and frame of a photo to make it look more appealing.

Sharpen and Reduce Noise: Use sharpening and noise reduction to improve image clarity and detail while reducing digital noise and artifacts. Sharpening sliders may be used to improve edge definition, and noise reduction settings can be fine-tuned to retain picture quality, particularly in low-light or high-ISO scenarios.

Experiment with Creative Effects: To add artistic flare to your images, try using vignetting, selective color tweaks, and graded filters. Use presets or custom modifications to create distinct appearances and styles that represent your creative vision.

Share your images: Once you've finished editing your images to your liking, it's time to show them off to the world. Consider sharing your photographs on social media sites like Instagram, Facebook, and Twitter to promote your photography and encourage people to visit Punta Cana. Use relevant hashtags, geotags, and descriptions to boost the exposure and engagement of your images.

Print and Display: By printing your best images from your Punta Cana trip, you can enjoy them in real form while also sharing them with friends and family. Consider producing picture albums, framed prints, or canvas prints to display your memories and relive your Punta Cana adventures.

By following these editing and sharing suggestions, you may improve the visual impact of your trip photographs and create lasting memories of your time in Punta Cana.

To summarize, photography is an effective technique for capturing the beauty and soul of Punta Cana, allowing visitors to save their memories and share their experiences with others. Explore the best photography spots, capture the essence of the destination, master smartphone and DSLR photography techniques, and edit and share your travel photos to create stunning images that will showcase Punta Cana's natural beauty, vibrant culture, and unique charm for years to come.

Chapter 19

TRAVELING WITH PETS TO PUNTA CANA

Traveling with pets may offer an added layer of enjoyment and companionship to your trip to Punta Cana, a tropical destination famed for its beautiful beaches and outdoor activities.

In this chapter, we'll go over everything you need to know about traveling with pets in Punta Cana, including pet-friendly accommodations, pet parks and outdoor areas, pet services and veterinary facilities, and travel safety precautions.

Pet-Friendly Accommodation Options.

Finding pet-friendly accommodations is the first step in organizing a trip to Punta Cana with your canine companion. Fortunately, many hotels, resorts, and vacation homes in

Punta Cana welcome pets, so you may spend your holiday together. Here are some pet-friendly accommodations in Punta Cana:

Pet-Friendly Hotels and Resorts: Many Punta Cana hotels and resorts have pet-friendly rooms and services for visitors who vacation with their dogs. These accommodations may feature pet-friendly rooms, pet-friendly regulations, and pet-friendly amenities like pet beds, food bowls, and welcome gifts.

Vacation Rentals: For additional room and solitude with your pet, consider renting a pet-friendly vacation house or villa in Punta Cana. Vacation rental websites like Airbnb and Vrbo let you filter search results by pet-friendly rentals, making it simple to discover the ideal home away from home for you and your furry buddy.

Pet-Friendly regulations: Before booking, consider the property's pet-friendly regulations, as well as any related costs or limitations. Some lodgings may have size or breed limits, pet fees, or special requirements for pet behavior and monitoring. Understanding and adhering to these standards is critical to ensuring a seamless and pleasurable stay for you and your pet.

Pet-friendly parks and outdoor spaces

Punta Cana has several parks and outdoor areas where you and your pet may enjoy the great outdoors together. There are lots of pet-friendly alternatives to choose from, whether you want to go for a scenic walk, play catch, or take a leisurely stroll along the beach. Here are several pet-friendly parks and outdoor venues in Punta Cana:

Juanillo Beach: This gorgeous stretch of shoreline in Punta Cana welcomes dogs. Take your dog for a walk along the immaculate sandy beach, let them play in the waves, or simply admire the ocean views together.

Punta Cana Ecological Reserve: The Punta Cana Ecological Reserve is a natural beauty preserve with trails and hiking pathways available for tourists to explore. Leashed pets are invited to accompany their owners on hikes within the reserve, where they may see local flora and creatures in their natural environment.

Los Corales Beach: Another pet-friendly beach in Punta Cana where you can enjoy the sun, sand, and sea with your canine companion. Take a leisurely stroll along the beach or sit beneath a palm tree while your pet explores the sandy landscape.

Dog Parks: While there are no official dog parks in Punta Cana, many hotels and resorts with pet-friendly policies have on-site dog parks or designated pet exercise areas where your pet may run and play off-leash in a safe and regulated setting.

Pet Services and Veterinary Clinics.

It's important to have access to pet services and veterinary clinics while traveling with pets in Punta Cana to guarantee their health and safety. Here are various pet services and veterinary clinics in Punta Cana:

Veterinarian Clinics: Punta Cana boasts a number of veterinarian clinics and pet hospitals that offer medical treatment, immunizations, and emergency services to pets. If your pet requires veterinary care during your visit, you can contact one of these clinics. Vet Point Bavaro and Vet Center Bavaro are two of Punta Cana's most prominent veterinary facilities.

Pet Supplies: If you need pet supplies or accessories during your trip, you may get them at pet stores and shops in Punta Cana. They provide a wide range of pet items such as food, toys, grooming supplies, and accessories. Some supermarkets and pharmacies may have basic pet supplies for your convenience.

Pet Grooming and Boarding: If you want to spend the day touring Punta Cana without your pet, you may book grooming or boarding services at local pet spas or kennels. These facilities include grooming, daycare, and overnight boarding alternatives for dogs, ensuring that they receive adequate care and attention while you are gone.

Safety Tips for Traveling with Pets

Traveling with dogs necessitates meticulous planning and preparation to ensure their safety and comfort throughout the trip. Here are some guidelines for traveling safely with dogs to Punta Cana:

Plan Ahead: Before coming to Punta Cana with your pet, look into pet-friendly accommodations, transportation alternatives, and local pet services to ensure a smooth and comfortable journey. Make prior bookings and check pet policies and costs with hotels, airlines, and car rental agencies.

Pack Essentials: Pack the essentials for your pet, such as food, water, bowls, meds, toys, bedding, and a leash or harness. Bring copies of your pet's immunization records, ID tags, and microchip information in case of an emergency.

Provide Comfort: Make your pet's travel environment as comfortable and familiar as possible by packing their favorite toys, blankets, and odors from home. For flight travel, use a safe and well-ventilated pet carrier or kennel, and provide plenty of time for exercise and toilet breaks on long automobile journeys.

Monitor Health and cleanliness: Throughout the journey, keep an eye on your pet's health and cleanliness, and treat any concerns or difficulties as soon as possible. Keep your pet hydrated, avoid feeding them unusual foods, and practice regular grooming and cleanliness to keep them comfortable and healthy when traveling.

Follow municipal rules: Learn about Punta Cana's municipal rules and leash restrictions to guarantee compliance and avoid fines or penalties. Respect the environment and other passengers by picking up after your pet and disposing of garbage correctly.

By following these pet travel recommendations in Punta Cana, you can guarantee that you and your animal companion have a safe, pleasurable, and memorable trip. Punta Cana welcomes guests and their dogs with open arms, offering pet-friendly accommodations, parks and outdoor areas, pet services, and veterinary facilities to help you create amazing moments in this tropical paradise.

Chapter 20

VOLUNTEERING AND COMMUNITY ENGAGEMENT OPPORTUNITIES

Volunteering and participating in community activities may be a wonderful way to give back and have a good effect while in Punta Cana.

In this chapter, we will look at the many volunteer and community involvement possibilities available in the region, such as local environmental conservation projects, social welfare efforts, cultural preservation programs, and voluntourism groups.

Local Environmental Conservation Projects

Punta Cana is home to a variety of habitats, including beautiful beaches, lush rainforest, and vivid coral reefs. Participating in local environmental conservation programs helps to preserve and safeguard these vital natural resources.

Here are some environmental protection initiatives in Punta Cana:

Beach Clean-Up Initiatives: Participate in beach clean-up events hosted by local conservation groups, hotels, and community organizations to help maintain Punta Cana's beaches clean and free of marine waste. Participating in beach clean-ups allows you to make a direct contribution to the conservation of marine habitats and species.

Coral Reef Monitoring: Take part in coral reef monitoring and restoration programs organized by marine conservation groups in Punta Cana. Collect data on coral health, monitor marine biodiversity, and aid in coral propagation and transplanting operations to repair damaged reef ecosystems.

Reforestation efforts: Participate in reforestation efforts to restore and preserve the natural ecosystems of Punta Cana's indigenous flora and wildlife. Plant trees, remove invasive species, and help with habitat restoration to boost biodiversity and minimize the consequences of deforestation.

Sustainable Agriculture Initiatives: Support sustainable agricultural efforts such as organic farming, agroforestry, and soil protection. Volunteer on organic farms, community gardens, or agroecological projects to learn about sustainable agriculture techniques and help to ensure food security and environmental sustainability.

Social Welfare Initiatives

Supporting social welfare activities allows you to positively touch the lives of local populations in Punta Cana. There are several methods to participate in social welfare programs, including assisting disadvantaged people, promoting education and healthcare, and supporting economic empowerment activities. Here are few examples:

Community Development Programs: Volunteer in Punta Cana's underprivileged neighborhoods to improve access to education, healthcare, housing, and basic services. Assist with building projects, educational seminars, health clinics, and other programs that aim to improve people's lives and promote social inclusion.

Orphanages and Children's Homes: Volunteer at orphanages and children's homes in Punta Cana, where you may provide care, assistance, and educational activities to orphaned and vulnerable children. Mentoring, tutoring, leisure activities, and arts and crafts projects may all help youngsters feel empowered and generate good experiences.

Senior Care Centers: Help senior care centers and nursing homes by offering your time and providing companionship to elderly people. Help plan recreational activities, social gatherings, and wellness programs to enhance physical and mental well-being among the community's elderly.

Animal Welfare groups: Participate in animal welfare groups and programs that encourage ethical pet ownership, animal rescue, and animal rights activism. Volunteer at animal shelters, take part in spay and neuter initiatives, and spread awareness about animal welfare concerns in Punta Cana.

Cultural Preservation Programs

Punta Cana's rich cultural legacy must be preserved and celebrated in order for local communities to keep their identity and customs. Participating in cultural preservation initiatives enables you to help protect traditional practices, heritage locations, and cultural expressions. Here are several cultural preservation projects in Punta Cana.

Indigenous Cultural programs: In Punta Cana, support indigenous cultural programs aimed at preserving and revitalizing indigenous traditions, languages, and cultural practices. Volunteer with indigenous communities to learn about their history, help with cultural events, and support projects that preserve indigenous knowledge and practices.

Historical Preservation projects: Participate in historical preservation projects aimed at saving and maintaining Punta Cana's historical landmarks, monuments, and heritage sites. Volunteer with heritage groups, museums, and historical societies to help with conservation, archival research, and educational activities.

Traditional Arts and Crafts programs: Take part in programs celebrating Punta Cana's cultural history. Learn traditional techniques including pottery making, weaving, and folk artwork from local artists and craftsmen, which will help to preserve traditional crafting skills and promote cultural exchange.

Cultural Festivals and Events: Support cultural festivals and events that celebrate Punta Cana's unique customs, music, dance, and food. Volunteer in cultural festivals, parades, and celebrations to help arrange and promote cultural activities, performances, and exhibitions for the enjoyment of both residents and tourists.

Volunteer Organizations and Opportunities

Voluntourism, also known as volunteer tourism, allows tourists to combine volunteering with travel, allowing them to have a good effect while seeing new countries and cultures. Voluntourism groups in Punta Cana enable visitors to participate in meaningful volunteer activities while discovering the beauty of the Dominican Republic. Here are a few volunteer groups and possibilities in Punta Cana:

Volunteer Abroad Programs: Participate in volunteer abroad programs run by respected organizations that provide volunteer opportunities in a variety of fields such as education, healthcare, conservation, and community development. These programs often provide volunteers with housing, meals, and support services, allowing them to make a significant contribution to local communities while immersing themselves in local culture.

Conservation excursions: In Punta Cana, take part in conservation excursions and eco-tours aimed at environmental conservation and wildlife protection. Join expert-led trips to isolated wilderness regions, national parks, and marine reserves to help with conservation research, habitat restoration, and animal monitoring.

Community Service initiatives: Participate in community service initiatives conducted by volunteer organizations to solve urgent social and environmental concerns in Punta Cana. Volunteer with local residents on projects including school building, clean water efforts, sustainable agriculture, and healthcare outreach programs.

Cultural Immersion Experiences: Learn about Punta Cana's culture and customs by helping with local communities on cultural preservation projects, historical conservation efforts, and traditional arts and crafts workshops. Volunteering allows you to learn about local communities' history, culture, and way of life while also having a constructive influence.

Participating in volunteer and community involvement options in Punta Cana allows you to support significant causes, connect with local communities, and create memorable memories of your trip.

Chapter 21

PUNTA CANA - PAST, PRESENT, AND FUTURE

Punta Cana, located on the Dominican Republic's eastern coast, has grown from a small fishing town to one of the Caribbean's top tourist attractions.

In this chapter, we'll look at Punta Cana's historical progression, contemporary socioeconomic situation, urban development initiatives, and efforts to preserve the city's legacy for future generations.

Historical Development of Punta Cana

Punta Cana's history extends back generations, with the indigenous Taino people being the first to settle the area. The Tainos subsisted on the land, fished in the plentiful rivers and growing crops like cassava, maize, and sweet potatoes. However, the entry of Spanish invaders in the 15th century resulted in a reduction of the Taino population owing to sickness, slavery, and forced labor.

Punta Cana has long been a sparsely inhabited and unspoiled location known for its coconut plantations, clean beaches, and lush tropical surroundings. Punta Cana did not see substantial expansion and development until the late twentieth century, which was fueled by the boom of Caribbean tourism.

In the 1970s, the Dominican government and international investors noticed Punta Cana's natural attractiveness and launched ambitious tourism development initiatives. Large-scale resorts, hotels, and golf courses were built along the beach, converting Punta Cana into a world-class tourist attraction.

The Current Socioeconomic Landscape

Today, Punta Cana is a major tourist destination, attracting millions of people each year with its gorgeous beaches, luxurious resorts, and vibrant culture. The tourist sector is critical to the region's economy, creating job opportunities, driving economic growth, and contributing to infrastructural development.

Hotels, resorts, restaurants, tour operators, transportation companies, and retail outlets all contribute to Punta Cana's tourist industry. These firms employ thousands of local inhabitants and make a substantial contribution to the region's GDP.

Despite its economic prosperity, Punta Cana has issues such as social inequality, environmental sustainability, and infrastructural development. Income gaps exist between tourist sector workers and the local population, with many inhabitants struggling financially and having limited access to education, healthcare, and basic amenities.

In Punta Cana, efforts are ongoing to solve these issues and encourage long-term development. Initiatives focusing on community empowerment, environmental conservation, and social inclusion seek to enhance inhabitants' quality of life while also ensuring equitable distribution of tourist benefits.

Urban Development Projects and Future Plans.

Punta Cana's urban development is constantly evolving, with continuous initiatives aiming at improving infrastructure, expanding tourism amenities, and boosting inhabitants' quality of life. Some important urban development projects and future planned are:

Infrastructure Improvements: Investments in roads, bridges, utilities, and public transit systems are critical to sustaining the booming tourism economy and boosting connectivity in Punta Cana and adjacent areas.

Sustainable tourist Development: In Punta Cana, there is a rising emphasis on sustainable tourist development, which includes reducing environmental impact, conserving natural resources, and encouraging responsible tourism practices. Sustainable tourism projects include environmentally friendly resorts, green building approaches, and environmental education programs.

Urban Planning and Design: Urban planning and design are critical to determining Punta Cana's future by ensuring that development is well-managed, ecologically sensitive, and socially inclusive. Smart growth concepts, mixed-use development, and pedestrian-friendly architecture are being used in urban planning to create lively, livable cities.

Economic Diversification: To minimize tourism dependency and encourage economic diversification, efforts are being made to attract investment in other areas like as agriculture, industry, technology, and renewable energy. Economic diversification programs seek to generate jobs, promote innovation, and lessen susceptibility to external shocks.

Protecting Punta Cana's Heritage for Future Generations

As Punta Cana grows and develops, keeping its legacy and cultural identity is critical to retaining the region's distinct charm and authenticity. Efforts to preserve Punta Cana's legacy for future generations include:

Cultural Conservation: Preserving traditional music, dance, food, and craftsmanship is critical to protecting Punta Cana's cultural legacy. Cultural conservation measures include assisting local craftspeople, encouraging traditional festivals and events, and recording oral histories and cultural customs.

Legacy Tourism: Heritage tourism programs seek to highlight Punta Cana's rich history and cultural legacy to guests, allowing for cultural interchange and immersive experiences. Heritage tourism activities include guided tours of historic places, cultural performances, and visits to museums and cultural institutions.

Historical Preservation: Protecting historical landmarks, monuments, and archeological sites is critical to preserving Punta Cana's historical history. Historical preservation activities include the protection, restoration, and interpretation of cultural heritage assets to guarantee their integrity and value for future generations.

Community Engagement: Involving local communities in history preservation efforts promotes pride, ownership, and management of Punta Cana's cultural legacy. Community-based initiatives allow locals to engage in decision-making, advocate for cultural protection, and pass down traditional knowledge and skills to future generations.

By protecting Punta Cana's heritage for future generations, the region can remain a lively and sustainable destination that embraces its cultural variety, natural beauty, and rich history. Punta Cana can strike a balance between growth and preservation by working collaboratively with government agencies, corporate sector players, and local communities to ensure a bright and successful future for future generations.

Chapter 22

CONCLUSION: EMBRACING PUNTA CANA'S CHARM

As your trip to Punta Cana draws to a close, it's time to reflect on the memorable experiences, magnificent scenery, and lively culture that have grabbed your heart.

In this last chapter, we send a warm farewell to Punta Cana, reflect on your Punta Cana experience, explore how to continue your trip beyond Punta Cana, and encourage you to share your Punta Cana experiences with the world.

Fond farewell to Punta Cana.

As you prepare to leave Punta Cana, take a minute to cherish the memories you've made during your stay in this tropical paradise. Whether you spent your days relaxing on sun-kissed beaches, exploring beautiful jungles, or immersing yourself in local culture, Punta Cana made an unforgettable impression on your spirit.

As you say goodbye to Punta Cana, remember to be grateful for the experiences, friendships, and joyful moments you've had along the road. Before saying farewell, take one more stroll down the coastline, breathe in the salty sea air, and appreciate the natural beauty of Punta Cana.

Though you are physically departing Punta Cana, the experiences and connections you have made here will last a lifetime. Carry the spirit of Punta Cana in your heart as you start on your next trip, knowing that you'll always have a piece of this magnificent place with you.

Reflection on Your Punta Cana Experience

As you reminisce on your Punta Cana vacation, consider the moments that made an indelible effect on you. Perhaps the bright hues of a Caribbean sunset, the rhythmic pulse of merengue music, or the warm smiles of the locals moved your spirit.

Consider the lessons and insights you've gathered over your stay in Punta Cana. Perhaps you've realized the value of living in balance with nature, celebrating cultural variety, or finding delight in simple pleasures. Consider how these encounters have enhanced your life and influenced your worldview.

Take the opportunity to write or share your thoughts with loved ones, preserving the spirit of your Punta Cana trip in words and memories. By capturing your experience, you'll be able to relive and treasure these memories for years to come, preserving the spirit of Punta Cana in your heart.

Continue Your Journey Beyond Punta Cana

As you say goodbye to Punta Cana, realize that your trip does not finish here. The world is filled with limitless opportunities, and there are other experiences waiting to be found beyond the sands of Punta Cana.

Consider where your travels will take you next, and enjoy the thrill of discovering new places, cultures, and experiences. Whether you're planning your next tropical vacation, traveling on a cultural trip, or seeking adventure in the great outdoors, let the spirit of adventure lead you.

Carry the lessons, memories, and experiences you learned in Punta Cana with you as you continue your trip. Let the beauty of Punta Cana inspire you to seek out new adventures, take on new challenges, and develop a greater appreciation for the world's beauties.

Share Your Punta Cana Memories.

As you think on your Punta Cana trip, consider how you may share your experiences and thoughts with others. Sharing your Punta Cana adventures, whether via narrative, photography, or social media, helps you to inspire and connect with other visitors from all over the world.

Share your best photographs, tales, and suggestions from your stay in Punta Cana on social media sites like Instagram, Facebook, and Twitter. Use hashtags like #PuntaCana, #TravelMemories, and #CaribbeanAdventure to reach a larger audience and encourage people to visit Punta Cana for themselves.

Consider writing a travel blog or making a picture album to commemorate your Punta Cana trip and share your experiences, insights, and suggestions with other visitors. By sharing your experiences and tips, you will not only preserve your memories but also assist others in planning their own great excursions in Punta Cana.

Finally, when you bid farewell to Punta Cana and embark on your trip beyond this tropical paradise, remember to treasure the experiences, lessons, and relationships you made throughout your stay. Take the spirit of Punta Cana with you wherever you go, knowing that the beauty and charm of this location will always have a special place in your heart. Farewell, Punta Cana, until we meet again.

APPENDIX

USEFUL RESOURCES

This appendix contains a variety of valuable materials to help you have a more pleasurable vacation to Punta Cana. These resources, which include emergency contact information, navigational tools, extra reading recommendations, and handy local phrases, will help you make the most of your visit in this tropical paradise.

Emergency Contacts:

It is critical to have emergency contact information while visiting Punta Cana. Knowing who to contact in a crisis might be the difference between getting medical help, police aid, or other emergency services. Here are some key emergency contacts in Punta Cana:

Emergency Services: Dial 911 if you need emergency police, fire, or medical help.

Medical Emergencies: If you have a medical emergency, contact your nearest hospital or clinic. Hospitals like Hospiten

Bavaro and Centro Médico Punta Cana provide emergency medical services.

Tourist Police: The Tourist Police in Punta Cana aid tourists in distress or during an emergency. You can contact the Tourist Police at +1 (809) 552-0635.

Embassy or Consulate: If you need assistance as a foreign traveler in the Dominican Republic, contact your country's embassy or consulate.

Maps and Navigation Tools

Maps and navigational aids make it easy to navigate Punta Cana and the surrounding areas. Whether you prefer classic paper maps or modern navigation tools, having access to dependable maps will allow you to explore with confidence. Below are some handy maps and navigational aids for Punta Cana:

Google Maps: www.google.com/maps - Google Maps provides detailed maps, driving instructions, and real-time traffic updates, making it an excellent tool for getting about Punta Cana and planning your travels.

Maps.me: www.maps.me - Maps.me is a smartphone app that offers offline maps of Punta Cana and other places, allowing you to travel without an online connection. Download the Punta Cana map ahead of time to have it available offline

Punta Cana Resort Maps: Many resorts and hotels in Punta Cana give extensive maps of their premises, including amenities, restaurants, and recreational areas. Check with your lodging provider for resort-specific maps and information.

Additional Reading and References

For individuals looking for more knowledge and insights into Punta Cana's history, culture, and attractions, extra reading materials and references might give context and inspiration. Here are some recommendations for books, websites, and resources:

Lonely Planet Dominican Republic (Travel Guide): www.lonelyplanet.com/dominican-republic - Lonely Planet's travel guide to the Dominican Republic includes detailed information on Punta Cana's attractions, lodging, food alternatives, and travel recommendations.

Punta Cana Travel Blog: www.puntacanatravelblog.com - The Punta Cana Travel Blog provides useful travel ideas, local perspectives, and recommendations for enjoying Punta Cana and its surroundings.

"**The Tainos:** Rise and Decline of the People Who Greeted Columbus" by Irving Rouse: This book delves deeply into the history and culture of the indigenous Taino people who formerly inhabited the Caribbean, including the area now known as Punta Cana.

"**The Rough Guide to the Dominican Republic" by Rough Guides:** (www.roughguides.com) - This comprehensive guidebook provides complete information on Punta Cana's sights, activities, lodgings, and practical travel tips.

Useful Local Phrases:

Learning a few simple Spanish words will improve your trip experience and allow you to converse with people in Punta Cana. While many workers in the tourist business understand English, knowing a few Spanish words might be handy in everyday situations. Here are some essential local terms to learn:

- Hola (Hello)

- ¿Cómo está? (How are you?)

- Gracias (Thank you)

- Por favor (Please)

- ¿Cuánto cuesta? (How much does it cost?)

- ¿Dónde está...? (Where is...?)

- No hablo español muy bien. (I don't speak Spanish very well.)

- ¿Puede ayudarme? (Can you help me?)

Practice these words before your vacation, and don't be hesitant to use them when talking with Punta Cana people. Your attempts to communicate in Spanish will be appreciated, and they can lead to more meaningful interactions and cultural experiences.

Addresses and Locations for Popular Accommodation

When arranging your vacation in Punta Cana, make sure to select accommodations that fit your interests and budget. From magnificent beachfront resorts to quaint boutique hotels, Punta Cana has a variety of lodging alternatives to meet the demands of every tourist. The following are the addresses and locations of prominent accommodations in Punta Cana:

Punta Cana Resort and Club

Address: Punta Cana Resort & Club, Punta Cana, Dominican Republic.

Site: www.puntacana.com.

Hard Rock Hotel and Casino Punta Cana

Address Blvd. Turístico del Este, Km. 28No.74, Macao, Dominican Republic.

Site: www.hardrockhotelpuntacana.com.

Barcelo Bávaro Grand Resort

Address: Carretera Bávaro km. 1. Playa Bávaro, Dominican Republic.

Web address: www.barcelo.com.

Excellence Punta Cana

Address: Playas Uvero Alto, Punta Cana, Dominican Republic.

Website address: www.excellenceresorts.com

Iberostar Grand Bávaro

Address: Carretera Arena Gorda, Playa Bávaro, Dominican Republic.

Web address: www.iberostar.com.

Majestic Colonial Punta Cana

Address: Carr. El Macao – Arena Gorda, Punta Cana, Dominican Republic

Visit www.majestic-resorts.com.

Dreams Punta Cana Resort and Spa

Address: Playas Uvero Alto, Punta Cana, Dominican Republic.

Site: www.dreamsresorts.com.

Secrets Cap Cana Resort and Spa

Address: Blvd. Zone Hotelera, Playa Juanillo, Cap Cana, Dominican Republic.

Website: www.secretsresorts.com.

Now Larimar, Punta Cana

Address: Ave. Alemania S/N, El Cortecito, Bavaro, Punta Cana, Dominican Republic.

Website address: www.nowresorts.com

The breathtaking Punta Cana Resort & Spa

Address: Playas Uvero Alto, Punta Cana, Dominican Republic.

Website: www.breathlessresorts.com.

Addresses and Locations of Popular Restaurants and Cafes.

Exploring the food scene is vital for discovering Punta Cana's colorful culture. From local Dominican food to worldwide cuisines, Punta Cana has a wide range of restaurants and cafés to suit every taste. The following are the addresses and locations of popular restaurants in Punta Cana:

La Yola Restaurant

Address: Punta Cana Resort & Club, Dominican Republic.

Visit www.puntacana.com/dining/la-yola.

Balicana Asian Cuisine

Address: Plaza Bávaro Shopping Center, Punta Cana, Dominican Republic.

Website address: www.balicanarestaurant.com

Jellyfish Restaurant

Address: Carretera Bavaro, Punta Cana, Dominican Republic.

Website address: www.jellyfishrestaurant.com

Bamboo Beach Club and Restaurant

Address: Carretera Bavaro, Punta Cana, Dominican Republic.

Site: www.bamboobeachclub.com.

Passion, by Martin Berasategui

Address: Paradisus Punta Cana Resort, Punta Cana, Dominican Republic.

Visit www.melia.com/en/hotels/dominican-republic/punta-cana/paradisus-punta-cana/passion-by-martin-berasategui.html.

Huracan Cafe

Address: Playa Bávaro, Punta Cana, Dominican Republic.

Website address: www.huracancafe.com

Captain Cook Restaurant

Address: El Cortecito, Punta Cana, Dominican Republic.

Website address: www.captaincookrestaurant.com

Citrus Restaurant

Address: El Cortecito, Punta Cana, Dominican Republic.

Website address: www.citrusrestaurantpuntacana.com

Casita de Yeya

Address: Carretera Verón-Punta Cana, Punta Cana, Dominican Republic.

Website address: www.lacasitadeyeya.com

El Fogon de La Abuela

Address: Avenida Estados Unidos, Bávaro, Punta Cana, Dominican Republic.

Website address: www.elfogondelaabuela.com

Addresses and Locations of Popular Bars and Clubs.

Punta Cana comes alive after dark with its dynamic nightlife scene, which includes a variety of bars, clubs, and entertainment venues where you can dance the night away and sip tropical drinks. The following are the addresses and locations of prominent pubs and clubs in Punta Cana.

Coco Bongo Punta Cana

Address: downtown Punta Cana, Dominican Republic.

Website address: www.cocobongo.com

Imagine Punta Cana.

Address: Imagine Plaza in Punta Cana, Dominican Republic.

Website address: www.imaginepuntacana.com

Drink Point

Address: Plaza Real Bávaro in Punta Cana, Dominican Republic.

Oro Nightclub

Address: Hard Rock Hotel & Casino Punta Cana, Macau, Dominican Republic.

Website: www.hardrockhotelpuntacana.com/nightlife/oro-nightclub.

Legacy Disco

Address: downtown Punta Cana, Dominican Republic.

Soles Chillout Bar

Address: Carretera Bavaro, Punta Cana, Dominican Republic.

Mangu Disco

Address: Carretera Arena Gorda, Punta Cana, Dominican Republic.

El Kan Drinking House

Address: Plaza Bibijagua in Punta Cana, Dominican Republic.

Aqua Lounge

Address: downtown Punta Cana, Dominican Republic.

Gabriela Bar and Lounge

Address: Playa Bávaro, Punta Cana, Dominican Republic.

Addresses and Locations of Major Attractions

Punta Cana is known for its breathtaking natural beauty, clean beaches, and a variety of sights and activities for visitors to enjoy.

Punta Espada Golf Club

Address: Cap Cana, Punta Cana, Dominican Republic.

Website address: www.puntaespadagolf.com

Indigenous Eyes Ecological Park and Reserve.

Address: Punta Cana Resort & Club, Dominican Republic.

Website: www.puntacana.com/indigenous-eyes-ecological-park.

Hoyo Azul

Address: Scape Park, Cap Cana, Punta Cana, Dominican Republic.

Website: www.scapepark.com/hoyo-azul.

Macao Beach

Address: Macao, Punta Cana, Dominican Republic.

Dolphin Island Park

Address: Bavaro, Punta Cana, Dominican Republic.

Website address: www.dolphinislandpuntacana.com

Saona Island

Address: Various departure locations in Punta Cana, Dominican Republic.

Website address: www.saonaisland.org

Los Haitises National Park

Address: Samaná Peninsula, Punta Cana, Dominican Republic.

Scape Park at Cap Cana

Address: Cap Cana, Punta Cana, Dominican Republic.

Website: www.scapepark.com.

Bavaro Beach

Address: Playa Bavaro, Punta Cana, Dominican Republic.

Horseback Riding at Uvero Alto.

Address: Uvero Alto, Punta Cana, Dominican Republic.

Snorkeling and Diving

Various sites along Punta Cana's coastline

Deep Sea Fishing

Departure locations vary; Punta Cana, Dominican Republic.

Website: (Local charter companies provide deep sea fishing trips)

Catamaran and Boat Tours

Departure locations vary; Punta Cana, Dominican Republic.

Parasailing and Jet Skiing

Various sites along Punta Cana's coastline

Kiteboarding and windsurfing

Various sites along Punta Cana's coastline

Visit to indigenous villages.

Departure locations vary; Punta Cana, Dominican Republic.

Local Art and Craft Markets

Plaza Bibijagua in Punta Cana, Dominican Republic

Dominican Cuisine Cooking Classes

Various places in Punta Cana, Dominican Republic.

Merengue and Bachata Dance Lessons

Various places in Punta Cana, Dominican Republic.

Cigar Rolling Workshops

Various places in Punta Cana, Dominican Republic.

Map of Punta Cana, Dominican Republic

https://maps.app.goo.gl/8sWU6A1NeX3x9kBZ6

SCAN IMAGE / QR CODE WITH YOUR PHONE

TO GET THE LOCATIONS IN REAL TIME

Map of Restaurants

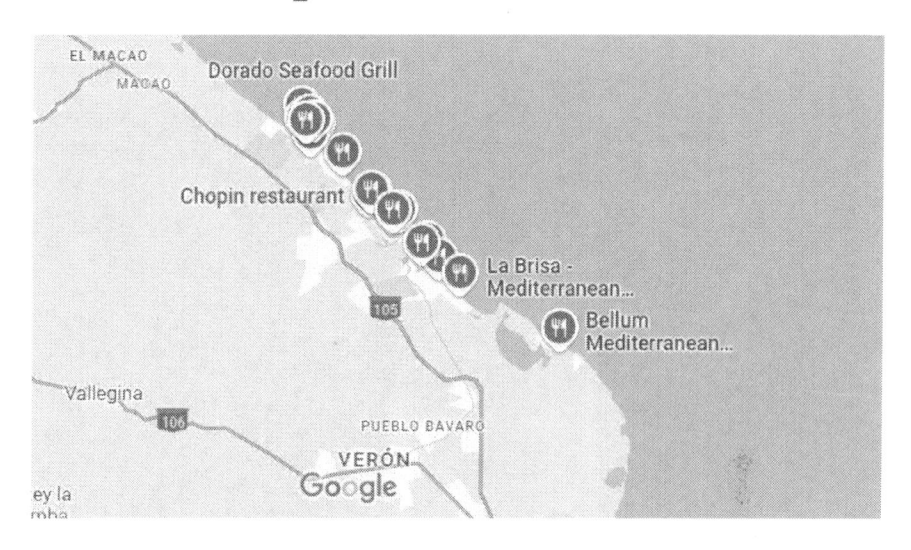

https://maps.app.goo.gl/z1K4cKY5n2SJksij9

SCAN IMAGE / QR CODE WITH YOUR PHONE

TO GET THE LOCATIONS IN REAL TIME

Map of Things to Do in Punta Cana

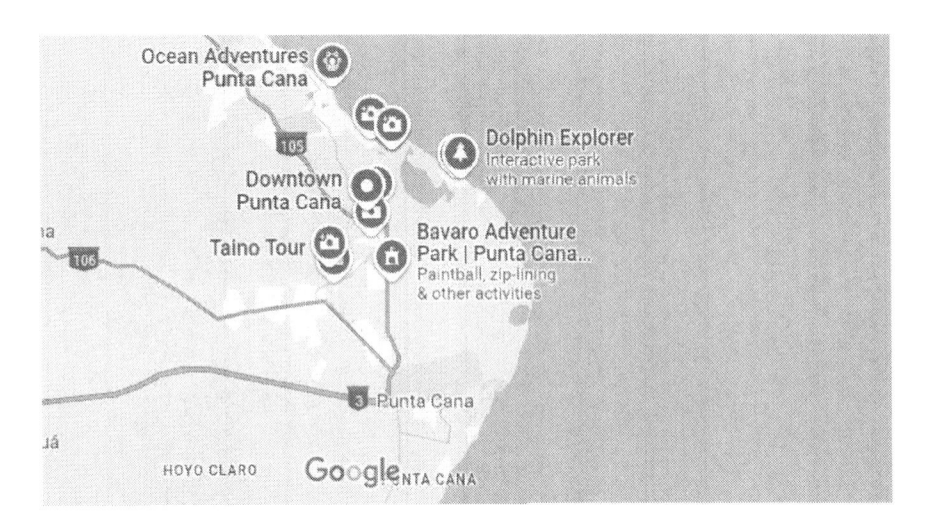

https://maps.app.goo.gl/eHLTNWuthPUvNVg37

SCAN IMAGE / QR CODE WITH YOUR PHONE

TO GET THE LOCATIONS IN REAL TIME

Map of Museums

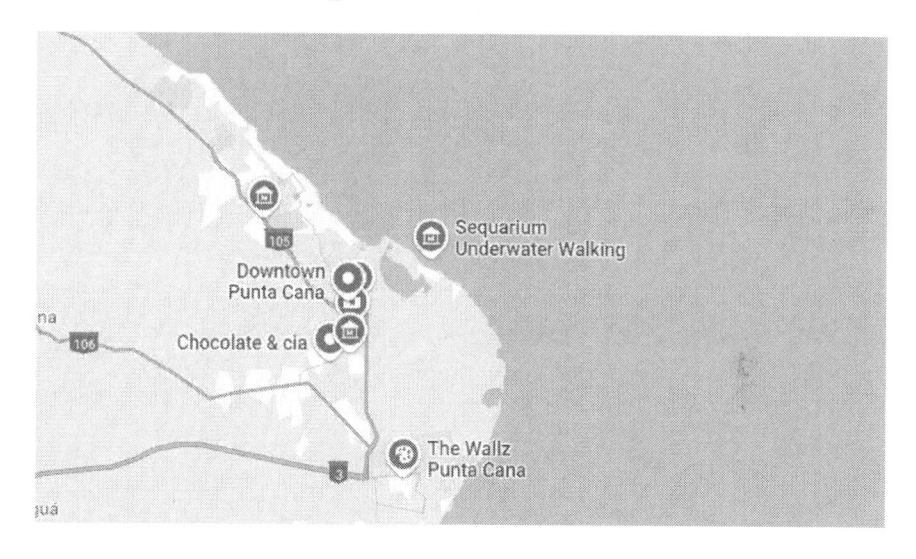

https://maps.app.goo.gl/HWXzaP7YtpGRxtAw7

SCAN IMAGE / QR CODE WITH YOUR PHONE

TO GET THE LOCATIONS IN REAL TIME

Printed in Great Britain
by Amazon